CONTENTS

Gotham Comes of Age

New York Through the Lens of the Byron Company, 1892–1942

by Peter Simmons

Museum of the City of New York

Pomegranate

San Francisco

The Museum of the City of New York is a nonprofit, private educational agency established in 1923 to collect, preserve, and present original materials related to the history of New York City. In addition to individual contributions and gifts from foundations and corporations, the Museum receives public funds from the New York State Council on the Arts, the National Endowment for the Humanities, and federal agencies. The City of New York, the Museum building's owner, provides support in the form of operating and programmatic funds through the Department of Cultural Affairs.

Museum of the City of New York
1220 Fifth Avenue
New York, New York 10029
(212) 534-1672
www.mcny.org

Published by Pomegranate Communications, Inc.
Box 6099, Rohnert Park, California 94917

Pomegranate Europe Ltd.
Fullbridge House, Fullbridge
Maldon, Essex CM9 4LE, England

Catalog No. A941
ISBN 0-7649-0906-1

This book was published on the occasion of the exhibition *Gotham Comes of Age: New York Through the Lens of the Byron Company*, at the Museum of the City of New York, April 17 through September 26, 1999. The exhibition was made possible in part by grants from the Metropolitan Life Foundation and Mr. and Mrs. Kenneth Lissak.

The photography for the plates was done by David Lubarsky Photography, New York; for the figure illustrations, by Victor Petryakov.

Library of Congress Cataloging-in-Publication Data
Simmons, Peter, 1964–
    Gotham comes of age : New York through the lens of the Byron
Company, 1892–1942 / by Peter Simmons.
        p.   cm.
    "Published on the occasion of the exhibition Gotham Comes of Age:
New York Through the Lens of the Byron Company, at the Museum of the
City of New York, April 14 through September 26, 1999"—T.p. verso.
    Includes bibliographical references (p. 210) and index.
    ISBN 0-7649-0906-1 (pbk.)
    1. New York (N.Y.)—History—1898–1951—Pictorial works—
Exhibitions. 2. New York (N.Y.)—History—1865–1898—Pictorial
works—Exhibitions. 3. New York (N.Y.)—Description and travel—
Exhibitions. 4. Byron Company (New York, N.Y.)—Exhibitions.
I. Museum of the City of New York. II. Title.
F128.5.S59 1999
974.7'1—dc21   98–47448
                                   CIP

Cover and interior design by Poulson/Gluck Design, Richmond, California

Printed in Hong Kong

08 07 06 05 04 03 02 01 00 99   10 9 8 7 6 5 4 3 2 1

The images of New York City found in the Museum of the City of New York's Byron Collection are visual testimonials to the rich fabric of urban life as the city emerged from the nineteenth into the twentieth century. The Byron photographs present the changing cityscapes that have made New York an exemplar of how cities are defined. We see the men, women, and children who inhabit this urban scene in all their wondrous diversity and complexity, working, playing, building, entertaining, healing, and protecting. Through the lens of the Byron camera we are welcomed into the homes of the rich and poor, into private clubs and public ballparks. At times it seems as if we are looking at another world. But as E.L. Doctorow notes in his introduction, we are attached to these people and this place through a shared urban memory. Everything is different and simultaneously familiar.

Peter Simmons, the Museum's Deputy Director for Collections Access and Publications, applied his considerable talents in the production of this book and the accompanying exhibition. In doing so, he has followed in the footsteps of Grace Mayer, the Museum's founding Curator of Prints and Photographs, who was the first to recognize the significance of the Byron Company's work. It is the Museum's hope that this catalogue and exhibition will remind New Yorkers and visitors to the city of the connections that bind the past and the present into the unfinished narrative of one of the most significant cities in history.

Robert R. Macdonald
Director
Museum of the City of New York

ACKNOWLEDGMENTS

For two years, beginning in 1993, I had the pleasure of managing a project funded by the National Endowment for the Humanities (NEH) to catalogue, re-house, and reproduce on microfiche the Museum of the City of New York's Byron Collection. This enlightening process was facilitated by two capable assistants, Eileen Kennedy and Diana Arecco, who spent day after day itemizing this collection of magnificent images. Eileen's continued presence at the museum has been a boon to me, and the luxury of her familiarity with the collection has often been taken for granted. Margaret Tamulonis, an intern for the NEH project, combed through files, city directories, and notes left behind by the Byrons, as well as by former Museum of the City of New York curators—most notably Grace M. Mayer—to gain a sense of the Byron Company's activities in New York.

Grace M. Mayer's copious Byron files document a nearly twenty-year relationship with the collection she acquired for the museum, and with the firm's final owner, Percy C. Byron. Without this body of knowledge, or her 1958 book, *Once Upon a City: New York from 1890–1910 as Photographed by Byron*, this catalogue would lack much of its historical context. Two books, produced in conjunction with the Museum of the City of New York by Dover Publications, have shaped the public perception of the Byron Company's work. They are *New York Life at the Turn of the Century* (1985, text by Albert K. Baragwanath), and *New York Interiors at the Turn of the Century* (1976, text by Clay Lancaster). Without ignoring this strong precedent, I have attempted to reveal the greater breadth of the Byron Company's work that was uncovered during our two-year NEH project.

In the preparation of this catalogue, I am most indebted to Carla Preston, who came to New York from London for a summer internship and was handed the terrific responsibility of researching more than 160 photographs. This book would not have been possible without Carla's impeccable research and her collaboration on its captions. Kathy Benson, the museum's editor, often turned babble into English, and her many readings of the text resulted in a far superior manuscript. Colleagues and friends whose comments helped to shape a better representation of New York City and the Byron Company include Bonnie Yochelson, Jan Ramirez, Alison Eisendrath, Haig Chahinian, Bob Shamis, Marguerite Lavin, and Rob Del Bagno. At Pomegranate, it has been a pleasure, as always, to work with publisher Katie Burke and managing editor James Donnelly.

Finally, and most fundamentally, I thank the Byron Company, with which I feel a strange and solid bond. Several descendants of the Byron photographers—including Pat Murtaugh, Bart Murtaugh, Laura Byron White, and photographer Tom Byron (who represents the sixth generation in the business)—have been consistently supportive of our work at the museum. The Museum of the City of New York is committed to making this remarkable body of work accessible to the broadest possible public, and has already made plans to place the Byron Collection, in its entirety, on the Internet for this very purpose.

Peter Simmons
Deputy Director for Collections
Access and Publications
Museum of the City of New York

E. L. DOCTOROW

*A*s they went about their business taking pictures of the realities of life in New York, the Byron photographers inadvertently recorded something else: an unsettling silence, perhaps, or the intimation in silver gelatin of our own mortality. Those men in derbies walking our streets, those women in long skirts and shirtwaists tending their children in our parks, those crowds standing on our docks, those strollers on Fifth Avenue and ice skaters in Central Park…they are not us, they are strangers inhabiting our city, though they are vaguely familiar, like the strangers in our dreams.

It is becoming clear that our ever changing, ever modern metropolis is in fact an older city, with ancient byways worn by the passage of generations. After all, with the exception of the Verrazano Bridge, our infrastructure was largely in place by the late thirties. The last of the major subway lines was built in the twenties. All the bridges and tunnels, and most of the roads and parkways as we know them, improved or unimproved, were completed by World War II. And going back even further, enormous evidence still stands of the nineteenth century—the Brooklyn Bridge, Central Park, the row houses of Harlem and Brooklyn, the ironfronts of Soho, for example. The city grid was laid out in the nineteenth century, so in

a sense, despite the activities or hyperactivities of our real estate magnates, we live to a surprising extent among the decisions of the dead.

It is an eerier, less populous city in the Byron photographs. Their commercially self-assured prints of dinner parties and street scenes produce in us a stillness that is like the stillness of listening to stories whose endings we already know. As if these are not images of past New Yorkers, but in the nature of the admonitory life of ghosts, to be of then and of now simultaneously, so as to hauntingly describe to us our membership in their world, granted just enough time for our illusions to flourish before we are chastened and subdued into our own places in the photographs.

By contrast, it may only be given to poetry, as for example Walt Whitman's, to assure us of the transcendent bustle and din, the overriding, exuberant arrogance of the living moment.

So of what may we be confident now, as the century ends? New York is a port, we mustn't forget that, a publishing hub, an electronics and communications center. It is a magnet for university intellects. It is the destination of the ambitious youth of the country. It is the capital of art, theater, literature, social pretension and subway tunnel home life. It is the capital of Napoleonic real estate mongers, grandiose rag merchants, self-important sports reporters, and statesmen who retire here to rewrite their lamentable accomplishments. It is the capital of people who make immense amounts of money without producing anything. It is the capital of people who work very hard and end up broke and grey. It is the capital of boroughs of vast neighborhoods of nameless drab apartment houses where genius is born every day. It is the capital of the contentious urban American mind that has never succumbed to a demagogue, a superpatriot, or a cleric who too confidently claims to speak for God.

It is the capital of all music. It is the capital of exhausted trees.

But it is also the capital of the dreams of the wretched of the earth. The problem New York poses for the rest of the country has finally to do with its cosmopolitan nature as contact city with the world's cultures, the challenge it is as an immigrant-infused megalopolis, to the creeds and complacencies that stultify our inland communities. New York is now, as it has been since the 1860s, a global city, the archetype city of everyone's future. People in every continent reason that if they can just reach our shore, they can scrabble up to a better life, or a more fighting kind of life where initiative can count for something. They will run newsstands or bodegas, or drive cabs, or peddle hot dogs, they will be janitors or security guards, whatever it takes.

Not that these remarks should be mistaken for romanticism. Every immigrant finds out quickly enough that freedom in America includes freedom to live under enormous stress. The fact is our vaunted diversity makes for trouble. Those who have come before traditionally give a hard time to those who have just come. Historically we are known for our riots and social disasters. The terrible racial fault line that goes through the heart of American society goes through our heart. The inequities of American society are visible in our schools and neighborhoods. The public discourse is degraded. The police force, which to serve society must be seen as honorable and fair, has lost the respect and trust of a large percentage of the population. And the underclasses gravitate to false prophets who teach them lies. All this is New York now—ethnic and social enclaves that are color coded, linguistically aggressive. We are these days a city of multicultural suspicions, as if the city as an idea is too much to bear even by the people who live in it.

And yet, if you find yourself on any street corner at the intersection of two busy streets, and imagine the action there frozen for a moment, you will reflect upon the thousands of lives going in all four directions, uptown downtown east and west, on foot, on bikes, on inline skates, in cars, trucks, buses, strollers, with the subway rumble underneath your feet …. and understand why you are momentarily part of the most spectacular phenomenon in the unnatural world. For all the alienation, the guarded privacy we maintain in our public spaces, in a very basic existential way we each rely on the masses of people around us to define ourselves. There is a kind of community oversoul, a species recognition that we will never acknowledge. The city as an idea may begin with the marketplace, the trading post, the confluence of waters, but it secretly depends on the human need to walk with strangers.

And so each of the passersby on this corner, every scruffy, oversized, undersized, weird, fat or bony or limping or muttering or foreign-looking, green-haired, punk-strutting, threatening, crazy, angry person you see…is a New Yorker, which is to say as native to this Diaspora as you are, and who must be acknowledged as such if we are not to become, even as we live, silver gelatinous ghosts among the ruins of a lost civilization.

FIGURE 1 The Byron family in Nottingham, England, 1888, just prior to the departure of Joseph, Julia, and Maude Mary to New York City. Left to right: Percy, Joseph, Georgiana, Maude Mary, Florence Mable, and Julia Lewin with baby Louis Philip. The Byron Collection, 93.1.4.1

THE BYRON COMPANY

OF NEW YORK CITY

PETER SIMMONS

*D*uring its 50-year tenure as one of New York City's preeminent commercial photography studios, the Byron Company witnessed and documented the maturation of the nation's great metropolis. Two major areas of specialization—stage and ship photography—provided steady work for the firm while it pursued thousands of other commissions that have contributed to the photographic legacy of New York City and the nation. The studio relied, over the years, on varying numbers of assistants and staff photographers, which always seemed to include members of the Byron family and their in-laws. Julia Lewin, wife of founder Joseph Byron, oversaw the studio's printing activities for roughly 40 years, and their children all participated in various roles, with their eldest son, Percy, making the business his life's work. Percy Byron's daughter Elizabeth, who served as his secretary from 1928 until 1935, represented the fifth generation of Byrons in the photography business.

The Byron Company traces its photographic roots to Nottingham, England, and the Clayton family, who, according to tradition, became involved in photography less than a decade after Louis Daguerre's and Henry Fox Talbot's first photographic discoveries.[1] James Clayton (1802–1863) is said to have opened a photographic studio in 1844, but the first verifiable existence of a family photographic establishment is in 1856, when James Clayton's son, Walter (1833–1893), opened his portrait gallery at 8 Greyhound Street, Long Row, Nottingham.[2] By 1857, Walter's brother, James Byron Clayton (1826–1880), had opened his own studio at 4 Ram Yard, Long Row East, operating under his baptismal second name Byron, so as to differentiate between his studio and that of his brother.[3] While the bulk of his business was portraiture, James's commissions also included copy-work of engravings and paintings, public and commercial buildings, and landscapes. This diversification of commissions and subject matter would persist in the work of James's son, Joseph Byron (1847–1923), in New York City. In 1870, the participation of Joseph Byron in his father's business was made official when the firm was renamed "Byron & Son."[4] After his father's death in 1880, Joseph maintained a photographic studio under the name "Joseph Byron." During this time, his wife, Julia Lewin, took an active part in the business, a role that would continue in New York City as she managed the studio's printing department.[5] With growing competition in Nottingham, and vast patronage opportunities in the burgeoning metropolis of New York City, the ambitious Joseph Byron set sail for America with his wife and eldest daughter, Maude Mary, in September 1888. They were joined in New York one year later by Byron's mother and the remaining children, including Joseph's future partner, Percy Byron (1878–1959).

After a year of press photography for the *Illustrated American* and miscellaneous free-lance projects, Joseph Byron embarked on what would be a 25-year career in stage photography. Using the flashlight method he had developed 20 years earlier in England, Byron became the first photographic artist of the stage. Up to this point, stage images had typically been drawn from life by artists—if they were produced at all—and the use of photography in theater advertisements and reviews had been limited to conventional portraiture. Joseph Byron described his flashlight method in a 1905 article entitled "American Flashlight Photography":

Nothing I did was entirely successful until I began using the magnesium powder, practically the only substance by which good flashlights can be obtained. When the magnesium powder is properly distributed, the result is a picture far more brilliant than any daylight photograph, for the simplest reason that you can get the light just where you want it. In taking flashlights of the stage I usually employ four men—one to look after the camera, and the other three to handle the lights. I know from experience just how a stage setting should appear in a photograph, and I am able to light up any corner or throw any part into the shade that I desire.[6]

Byron's mastery of flashlight photography, combined with his enterprising determination, initiated the expanded role of photography in the theater arts. Soon, stage photography would become a commonplace and competitive field. Initially, Byron talked his way past reluctant producers into dress rehearsals of productions, making prints and selling them to the daily newspapers. As his prints were published, producers began to recognize the publicity value of Byron's work, and he began to enjoy easy access at stage doors. Byron, with his son Percy, continued to photograph stage performances and personalities on speculation until about 1897, when burlesque producers Joseph Weber and Lew Fields commissioned the Byron Company to photograph the opening of the Imperial Music Hall at Broadway and 29th Street. Weber and Fields paid for the prints themselves, and gave them to the newspapers for publicity. This promotional activity set a new precedent for the business of theater photography, and from that time forward other play producers followed suit, bringing considerable security to the role of the photographer in the business. Another hurdle for Byron was to gain the confidence and respect of well-known theater personalities. One of Percy Byron's fondest memories was that of his father's getting permission to photograph Sarah Bernhardt in *Izeyl:*

After much trouble he got Sarah Bernhardt's permission to make a picture of her play— *Izeyl.* She said she would give him fifteen minutes in which to make it....She was so pleased she kissed me and said my father was a prince and that we must photograph all her plays, which we did. The *New York World* made a two-page spread of three of them.[7]

The first five years of the twentieth century were the most prolific and successful for the Byron Company's stage photography. Joseph Byron's 1915 recollection of the work emphasized the grueling, but clearly rewarding, nature of the business at that time:

Stage photographs are nearly always made under certain disadvantages—either at the full-dress rehearsal, which may run to three or four o'clock in the morning, or after the first performance on opening night, when the stage settings for the picture parts must be specially put on again. In either case, the players are tired, nervous, and high-strung, and the photographer, with all his manipulating and lighting to attend to, has also to reckon with the feelings of his subjects.[8]

Byron's photography of stage productions was an elaborate production in itself. While the finished product implies a direct and easily-acquired image of a performance, the process described in Joseph Byron's statement suggests the complexities involved.

Between 1900 and 1903, the Byron Company produced lantern slide shows based on their magnificent collection of stage photography. *Byron's Gigantic Illuminated Stage Pictures* were shown at theaters in New York City and other cities and towns around the country, with accompanying lectures by theater aficionados and historians. The *Boston Herald* of December 14, 1902, noted, "The pictures are of such mammoth proportions that they will fill the whole proscenium opening. They will be presented with an expert manipulation of light and color....The prices are to be popular." Byron's slide shows brought a taste of the theater to many who could not afford to attend or did not have access to live productions. This unintentional altruism was a positive side effect of the profit-driven enterprise. Byron's lantern slide presentations exploited photography's potential in the realm of popular entertainment. These slide shows, with their rapidly changing images suggesting a continuous production, can be compared with the fledgling film industry. Such an association with the moving image can be inferred from a description in the *New Bedford Morning Mercury* of May 8, 1903: "The views are changed rapidly, affording, with the reader's description, a clear idea of the play reproduced." Byron's lantern slide shows generally included about 200 images, covering several theatrical productions. Over the course of an engagement, which included a variety of shows, more than 1,000 different images would be projected for the enthusiastic audiences.

Through their work in the theater, Joseph and Percy Byron became part of the exclusive theater and arts community of New York City.[9] This insider status led to their producing several hundred portraits of stage celebrities, theater businesspeople, artists, and authors, including such luminaries as Maude Adams, Ethel Barrymore, David Belasco, Lillian Russell, and Mark Twain. Many of these portraits were taken in the sitters' homes and were usually composed to present the subject in a casual state. Joseph Byron reminisced in 1915 about his portraits of stage personalities: "It has been my privilege to see and photograph some of these actors not only on the stage but in their own apartments, and, in the case of several of the American artists, in their own family groups....Into many such homes have I been called with my camera, and some highly prized pictures are the results of those familiar visits."[10] The Byrons took advantage of their personal connection with their subjects, rejecting the rigid portraiture practiced by most photographers, including Joseph's father and uncle. Byron's unique style did not go unnoticed by contemporary critics.

FIGURE 2 Bill advertising *Byron's Gigantic Illuminated Stage Pictures* at the Lawrence [Massachusetts] Opera House. Museum of the City of New York.

Referring to Byron's portraits of "the leading personages in public life and of the theatrical profession," an article entitled "Progress in the Art of Photography" in the *Mercantile and Financial Times* noted: "The artistic results arrived at in this studio, still embody those most commendable features we have mentioned, to wit; the entire absence of the studied effect, and, consequent results which, by their entire naturalness of impression, appeal to the connoisseur as well as the ordinary observer."[11] Comparing Byron's portraiture to that of his predecessors and contemporaries reveals the radical difference between the static, posed portraits that had been the norm, and the unstudied, personal quality that Byron's familiarity with his subjects enabled him to achieve (figs. 3 and 4).

One of the Byron Company's most fortunate early commissions was that of P. F. Collier, publisher of *Once A Week* (later *Collier's Weekly*). Beginning in 1894, Collier hired the Byron Company to photograph the homes of New York's "400" (referring to New York City's 400 wealthiest citizens), one to be featured in his publication each week. This commission introduced the Byrons to yet another clientele in New York — one that would make much use of the publicity afforded by the Byrons' photographs. Percy Byron reminisced about the Collier commission and the studio's new-found popularity among members of New York society and those who sought inclusion in this set: "Of course you must get the very cream of the crop at the start, after that you need protection from the rest, they are so anxious to see their homes in the *Weekly*."[12] This account of the rich, desiring to publicize their wealth, suggests an underlying truth to social scientist Thorstein Veblen's 1899 *Theory of the Leisure Class,* wherein he states that "conspicuous consumption of valuable goods is a means of reputability to the gentleman of leisure."[13]

The Byrons' introduction to the "400" initiated a fruitful succession of society-related commissions, such as weddings, dinners, and excursions, around the turn of the century. Two significant commissions were the James Hazen Hyde Ball held at Sherry's Restaurant in 1905 and the Mark Twain dinner held at Delmonico's Restaurant in 1905 in honor of Twain's

FIGURES 3 AND 4 Sarah Bernhardt by the Byron Company with companion Suzanne Seytor at Bernhardt's Hoffman House apartment in 1896 (*above,* The Byron Collection, 41.420.529), and by Sarony, N.Y., c. 1880 (*right,* Theater Collection, Museum of the City of New York, 41.81.2).

70th birthday. The guests at the Hyde Ball represented the Byrons' society connections while those at the Twain dinner represented the artistic and literary side of the Byron studio's repertoire. The personalities that appeared in the photographs of these auspicious events resurfaced repeatedly in the Byron Company's work over the years.

E. Idell Zeisloft's *The New Metropolis* (D. Appleton & Co., 1899) is prolifically illustrated with photographs by the Byron Company. This 600-page, limited-edition volume celebrating the 1898 consolidation of New York's five boroughs took advantage of Byron's range of interests and clientele, from society events to theater, to street scenes on the Lower East Side. The nature of the Byron Company's association with

SARAH BERNHARDT

Sarony

37 UNION SQ. N.Y.

Zeisloft's project is not clear, but some of the published Byron Company images—such as the 1896 production of the play *Gismondia*—came from Byron's ample collection of New York City imagery, while other views, such as those of the Lower East Side and the group portrait of the Daughters of the American Revolution, all dated 1898, were most likely taken for the publication itself. The sheer volume of Byron Company photographs used in the book—roughly 80 percent of its total images—suggests that Byron was hired as the official photographer for the project.[14]

When the studio's schedule was not filled with commissions, the Byron Company sought out any news-related event that might sell. Percy Byron later recalled: "Until the plays and the steamships built up

into a full job, we covered most of the sports, indoors and out, blizzards and big banquets and all newsy [*sic*] events that we could reach....These news photos we sold to publishers in most of the countries all over the world."[15] Not all of the Byron Company's speculative news-photography ventures were successful. A *Journal of Photography* writer recollected in the January 19, 1900, issue:

> I was with [Joseph] Byron one winter day, when he—and I, too—stood all day in the bitter cold and blinding snow, at Lyndhurst-on-the-Hudson, to make a picture of Helen Gould when she should drive up to the castle door, on her return from the city. One hundred dollars was offered for this picture, but the reward was failure and two bad colds.

Regardless, the proliferation and variety of images that survive from the Byron Company confirms that the Byrons always managed to capture the limitless day-to-day events of New York City life.

While the bulk of their photographs were taken in New York City, approximately 15 percent of the Byron Company's work occurred outside the city limits. Most of these commissions came from established clientele who wanted their property or events away from the city captured on film. Examples include the country estates of F.G. Bourne, president of the Singer Sewing Machine Co. on Long Island (fig. 5), and of Miss Helen Gould, daughter of financier Jay Gould, whose Gothic style residence overlooked the Hudson River at Irvington, New York (fig. 6); a 1919 excursion of a group of hotel managers (most of whom had individually commissioned the Byron Company over the years) to the opening of the Hotel Griswold at New London, Connecticut; and the 1896 Democratic National Convention in Chicago, a commission from the *New York Journal* (fig. 7). Other non-New York images do not have such clear lineage, including views of the Panama Canal under construction (fig. 8), a dog sled in the "far north," and general views of Boston (fig. 9). One of the Byron Company's more interesting non-New York commissions took place during the Spanish-American War. In 1898, Percy was hired by the *New York Evening Journal* to join its reporting expedition aboard railroad magnate Henry M. Flagler's yacht, *Anita* (fig. 10):

> One late afternoon we were just off San Juan, Puerto Rico when two Spanish gunboats gave us chase, there was one comforting fact about these parts—twilight is of such short duration, it was soon dark, but they were gaining on us; we had a tubular boiler in our yacht, which is alright with hard coal, but we were loaded up with bituminous coal mostly all dust at that, and without forced draught you are a dead duck, so into our furnace went hams and bacon and what have you, then there was a lick of flame from our lone funnel about fifteen feet long, with that bright target they let go two shots just ahead of our bow, I heard no more, rushing off to the galley to get some food for as good an opportunity might not be mine again for a long time.[16]

The bulk and scope of non-New York images indicates that the Byron Company's influence—like that of New York City itself — spread far beyond the limits of the five boroughs.

In the spring of 1906, Percy Byron suddenly left the firm and New York City and relocated to western Canada, where his sister, Florence, and her new husband, Gustave May (they had married the previous year), lived. His reasons, as he recorded in his often sentimental memoir, written some 50 years later, included an adventurous wish to experience "the last great west that was opening in Canada." He also cited ill health: "I was far from well, too many long seasons of late or all night dress rehearsals, sometimes into another day but not a bed, and perhaps another night at the theater…"[17]

But it is likely that Percy was also dissatisfied with the nature of his work at the Byron Company. His father, Joseph, was president and the known entity of the studio, while Percy, although a stockholder, held the comparatively subordinate office of treasurer. While his father remained in the city, cultivating new business and maintaining the firm's good social standing with its established clientele, Percy traveled with studio employees to photograph out-of-town rehearsals. At age 27, Percy may have felt like a hireling in the family business; and he may have left for "the last great west" in the hope of achieving independence.

Ostensibly, Percy intended to lead a peaceful life as a

FIGURE 5
F.G. Bourne Residence, Oakdale, Long Island, 1900.
The Byron Collection, 93.1.1.9696

FIGURE 6 (*facing page*)
Miss Helen Gould Residence (the late Jay Gould residence), Lyndhurst, Irvington-on-Hudson, New York, 1894. The Byron Collection, 93.1.1.9977

homesteader and rancher. But within 24 hours of his arrival in Edmonton, Alberta, in April 1906, he had telegraphed his father with a request for photoengraving equipment. Recognizing the opportunities for a photographic business in the fledgling city, he established, in his words, "the first photo-engraving plant between Winnipeg and this side of the Pacific cities." A year later, he asked his brother-in-law, Gustave May, to be his business partner.

The prolific Byron-May Company enjoyed great success. Images produced by the company can be seen in most period tour books and pictorial descriptions of western Canada of the period, confirming its predominance in the scenic imagery market. A 1912 *Edmonton Bulletin* noted that the Byron-May Company had "secured a photograph of Alberta wheat fields, that is used continually for publicity purposes and has been the photographer of all the modern buildings and public episodes that has [sic] occurred here in recent years." However, the firm's mainstay was in the illus-

tration and design of product catalogues—a significant venture in the early days of product advertising. By 1913, the Byron-May Company had 16 employees, and May, who had been elected alderman in 1912, was a leader in the Edmonton community. Throughout his stay in Canada, Percy Byron continued to be listed in the New York City directories as the treasurer of the Byron Company. The Byron Company, in turn, was often listed in the same directories with its New York address (and Joseph as president) as well as a Canadian branch—the Byron-May Company—with Percy as the managing director, and Gustave May as secretary and treasurer.

As the effects of World War I penetrated the West, Percy Byron's and Gustave May's business in Edmonton declined. Percy recalled in his memoirs:

> The business grew immensely, but in 1914 when the war came it hit us very badly, no new money coming into the country, especially the

West....I lost quite a fortune but remembering what Henry Ford once said "Every man should fail before he's forty" and only being thirty-nine, thought well, I'm saved, but having been up and down that ladder so often decided if I could just stick about on a middle way that was about the best spot of them all, and having made a few trips each way I believe I should know.

Meanwhile, Joseph Byron had been sustaining the Byron Company in New York with a variety of commissions, including the company's mainstay—theatrical work. By this time, however, Joseph no longer had a virtual monopoly on the genre he had essentially invented. His sentimental concession to the presence of increasing competition was quoted in the December 25, 1915, *Bellman*:

Stage photography is as common now as any other kind of photography by artificial light.

I have long since ceased to be alone in the field. But I have my pictures. I value them because of the associations back of them. To have come into close relation with men like Irving and Belasco, and women like Sarah Bernhardt and Julia Marlowe, and all the rest, has been a privilege that has offset the difficulties I had at first, and the rich personality of this or that great dramatist remains in my recollections, even without the pictures. I have enjoyed being a stage photographer....[18]

The winner of several awards and medals for his stage and interior photographs, Joseph Byron could reflect upon his career with pride.

Upon his 1917 return to New York, 39-year-old Percy Byron began what would become the firm's second major specialization—ship photography. Percy's memoirs imply that this decision was made mutually with his father, and that it was in direct response to

FIGURE 7
Democratic
National
Convention,
Chicago, 1896.
The Byron Collection,
93.1.1.3989

FIGURE 8 Panama Canal Construction, Upper Lock, Lake Gatun, 1913. The Byron Collection, 93.1.1.7567

the grueling night work required of plays, dinners, and the like. But, judging from the state of Joseph's theater commissions, the time seems to have been right for Percy to play a more dominant role in the family business, perhaps determining its new direction. At this time, the studio also adopted a new method of recordkeeping: a ledger recording client, date, and a description of the subject for each negative. The negatives were cross-referenced in another ledger by subject. This ledger keeping represented a major change from the rudimentary listings that had been theretofore employed. Perhaps Percy's experience in Edmonton gave him the confidence and means to take on a new and more authoritative role in the Byron Company's business.

Ship photography was not new to the Byron Company, as it had photographed some 70 ships prior to 1917.

However, this new intentional concentration, championed by Percy, would result in the documentation of nearly every steamship to enter New York Harbor between 1917 and 1940. While theater photography was clearly Joseph's passion, Percy became the master of ship photography, carrying on the studio's new specialty well beyond his father's death in 1923. The proliferation of ocean liner commissions secured by the Byron Company after 1917 represented both Percy's avid interest and a dependable source of income for the studio. There were other clients during this time, but the bulk of the studio's work came from several large passenger ship lines, the most significant being the French Line. More than 350 images of that company's S.S. *Normandie* survive as a record of its maiden voyage, on which Percy Byron was the official photographer. Percy later recalled the tumultuous trip:

We [Percy and his assistant, Harry Blum] sailed back on the S.S. *Normandie*'s maiden voyage, for those four days I slept from 3 to 6 a.m. but at Quarantine I delivered 650 photographs. When boarding…we had 37 pieces of equipment which was right in our two large cabins and bathrooms….Everything from 35mm and 11×14 cameras, tripods, enlarger tanks, racks, developers and other chemicals, the trip and the results of hard work were a great success but I am sorry for those two bathrooms due to a fast and rough voyage much of the time…there was much spillage on the floor and sometimes we landed with a dish right up against the wall. I felt bad about all this but the Purser said back in Le Havre they would fix that like new in a little while, they must have done so for the next time she came in I was aboard and had my look and you would never think that a couple of slobs like ourselves had ever been in there.[19]

This description prompts one to wonder if in fact ship photography was less strenuous for Percy than the arduous theater work, and suggests that he had indeed found his true passion in photographing the great ocean liners.

FIGURE 9 Bird's-eye view of Boston, 1904. The Byron Collection, 93.1.1.1689

Percy ran the Byron Company after his father's death in 1923. The later work of the studio, consisting mostly of ship photography and a wide array of commercial documentation of the work place, architecture, and numerous organizations, reflects the technical prowess of Percy Byron. In the same way that the studio's earlier work reflects the influence of Joseph Byron's social connections and his often personal relationship with his subjects, Percy's work is a product of the highly structured, orderly environment of the machine age—instead of infusing his work with personality, this element is intentionally, and successfully, suppressed. Percy's mastery of composition and technique brought this work to its highest level, and resulted in several gold medals and other competition awards, including First Prize at the International Exposition in 1931 and 1932. When the available photographic tools were not sufficient to meet Percy's needs, he would dexterously invent and build the necessary equipment—a survival technique he learned from his father, who invented and built much of his own equipment, particularly while perfecting flashlight photography.

By the 1930s, the Byron Company was working almost exclusively in ship photography, and with the onset of World War II, its business waned. Percy Byron later lamented: "…[shipping] lines had no Atlantic service to sell to the regular run of passengers; everything was in the service of the war…they did not need my pretty pictures to sell passage over the Atlantic when just government alone will buy every footage of every craft…"[20] Again, a world war had frustrated Percy Byron's continued success. The Byron Company, Inc., filed a certificate of dissolution with New York's Secretary of State on October 5, 1942.

That same year, Percy donated the bulk of the firm's photographic archives, numbering approximately 20,000 prints and negatives, to the Museum of the City of New York. Several smaller donations followed over the next 16 years—a period when Grace M. Mayer, the museum's curator of prints, forged a lasting friendship and professional relationship with Percy. Mayer mounted several exhibitions based on the Byron Collection—*New York Half a Century Ago* (1949), *Out of My Files* (1951), and *All Indoors*

(1953), to name a few—but her magnum opus was her tale of New York City from 1890 to 1910 as photographed by the Byron Company. The 511-page *Once Upon a City*, published by the Macmillan Company in 1958, familiarized the world with Byron's photographs, and was augmented by Mayer's extraordinarily well-researched and enchanting narrative. Much of the great Byron legacy that continues to this day began with Mayer's *Once Upon a City*.

Six months after closing the Byron Company's West 54th Street studio, 64-year-old Percy Byron—not one to be idle—went to work for the Art Engraving Company of Newark, New Jersey. He was grateful to be busy, but noted, "it is not what I would call work, it is just enough to keep your motor turning over and your brain from getting lazy."[21] With declining health, and having seen *Once Upon a City* come to fruition, Percy Byron retired in December 1958, and died at the age of 80 on June 10, 1959.

NOTES

1. A thorough history of the Clayton/Byron family prior to Joseph Byron's emigration to New York in 1888 was written by Bernard V. and Pauline F. Heathcote, "The Clayton (Byron) Family in England," *History of Photography*, 9:1 (January-March 1985).

2. Heathcote, p. 57

3. ibid., p. 62

4. ibid., p. 68

5. ibid., p. 70

6. "American Flashlight Photography: Mr. Byron and His Work," *The King* (November 18, 1905), p. 187

7. "Autobiographical notes made by Percy C. Byron, 1953," typescript, Museum of the City of New York

8. Aubrey Fullerton, "Recollections of a Stage Photographer," *The Bellman* (December 25, 1915), p. 719

9. Percy Byron's memoirs attribute the studio's theater work largely to his father. Joseph was clearly the one with a passion for the theater, and the well-connected socialite of the firm. However, until he left for Canada in 1906, Percy was an integral part of the firm, and was a full participant in their theater-related work.

10. Fullerton, p. 724

11. From a clipping on file at the Museum of the City of New York. No date is associated with the clipping, but the published address of the Byron Studio places the article after but near the turn of the century.

12. Notes made in 1953 by Percy Byron regarding various commissions. Museum of the City of New York.

13. *The Columbia Dictionary of Quotations*, Columbia University Press, New York, 1993

14. Unlike work by other artists and photographers published in the book, the Byron photographs in *The New Metropolis* are never credited to the Byron Company, and the publisher claimed copyright ownership of all unattributed pictures, further suggesting the Byron Company's official capacity.

15. Notes made by Percy Byron, n.d.; housed at the Museum of the City of New York.

16. Percy Byron memoir, manuscript, 31 pp., c. 1955. Museum of the City of New York.

17. ibid.

18. Fullerton, p. 720

19. Percy Byron memoir.

20. ibid.

21. ibid.

Percy C. Byron by David C. McLane, 1953.
Museum of the City of New York, 93.1.4.25 Gift of *The News*.

GOTHAM COMES *of* AGE

The following images were selected from the Museum of the City of New York's Byron Collection, which includes more than 22,000 vintage prints and negatives produced by the Byron Company. The bulk of the collection was donated to the museum by Percy Byron in the years following the firm's closing in 1942. Several hundred additional works have found their way to the museum through other generous donors whose New York collections naturally included Byron Company photographs.

Most of the vintage prints in the Byron Collection are on single-weight printing-out paper, and have a rich brown to purple hue. Some of the prints—particularly those dating after about 1915—are the more typical and familiar silver gelatin prints. With few exceptions, the images are contact prints from 8×10 inch or 11×14 inch glass-plate and film negatives, resulting in exceptional detail and sharpness.

Because it is rarely known for certain who was behind the camera at any given moment, the images are simply and appropriately credited to the Byron Company. Captions refer to "Byron" in a generic way, though some instances lend confidence to a more specific attribution to either Joseph or Percy Byron. The Byron Company was a commercial firm that responded to the needs and demands of its clients and of speculative ventures. That the firm's technique and ability resulted in such an extraordinary body of work is a tangential benefit for today's viewers.

Wherever possible, titles of prints are those bestowed by the Byron Company. The studio often scratched titles into the emulsion of a negative, leaving a permanent identification. Other titles have been gleaned from Byron Company descriptions on negative and print envelopes, from a list of subjects photographed prior to 1917, and from a formal ledger maintained after 1917.

This sampling of the Byron Company's portfolio includes the familiar and expected, as well as never-before-published images. It is meant to evoke New York City during its coming of age as the world's great metropolis and to represent the tremendous scope of work covered by the Byron Company over its fifty-year career. It does not reflect the true proportions of Byron's many subjects; that would have left a selection heavily weighted toward the company's most successful areas—the theater and steamships—which make up about 50 percent of the collection. These, and several other categories of the Byron Company's work, merit exploration and publication in and of themselves.

STREET LIFE

The swirling currents that lave the shores
of Manhattan Island, flowing in every direction,
are reproduced in the human currents that eddy
and rush through the streets of New York.

FRANK MOSS
THE AMERICAN METROPOLIS, 1897

Through a combination of fortunate commissions and a clear natural attraction to the frenetic everyday life of the city, the Byron Company amassed an unparalleled document of New York's street life. Much of this work was done under the auspices of Idell Zeisloft's *The New Metropolis,* a limited edition volume celebrating the 1898 consolidation of Greater New York. Unlike most commercial commissions, which require very specific subjects, this opportunity allowed Byron to capture many general aspects of city life.

Even in photographs with a relatively mundane and specific subject, Byron had a keen ability to catch the eye. Many of the Byron Company's photographs cannot be clearly linked to a specific client, and it is reasonable to assume that sometimes there was no client. The Byrons obviously enjoyed their art, and would take photographs for the pleasure of it, always with the hope of finding an interested buyer. In the firm's later years Byron's signature New York street scenes gave way to more specialized work.

MOTT AND PARK STREETS, C. 1900

THE BYRON COLLECTION, 93.1.1.24448

At the junction of Mott and Park Streets—once the worst slum area in New York City—these Lower East Side immigrants work and play in the shadow of an American Express Company office. American Express, founded in 1850 for parcel post service between New York and California, provided two essential services to the local immigrant community: currency exchange for those who had recently passed through Ellis Island, and money orders for sending money to friends and family back home.

HERALD SQUARE, c. 1906

This view looking south along Broadway from 36th Street captures Herald Square—named for the newspaper headquartered there from 1893 until 1921—in its infancy as a world-famous shopping district. Shoppers abound and a barker for Healy's joins a newspaper vendor trying to capture customers as the sun dips in the late afternoon.

HESTER STREET — JEWISH QUARTER, 1898

THE BYRON COLLECTION, 93.1.1.15360

Views similar to this image were published in *The New Metropolis* with the conscious goal of documenting one of New York's major ethnic neighborhoods—the "Jewish Quarter." According to *The New Metropolis*, approximately 1,500 Lower East Side families, with an average family income of $5 per week, depended on the Hester Street Market as their main source of food. This area of lower Manhattan is still home to many Jewish-owned businesses.

OPPOSITE MULBERRY BEND, N.Y., 1898

THE BYRON COLLECTION, 93.1.1.17141

This stretch of East Broadway was enjoying a revival of sorts after the 1892 demolition of the adjacent notorious slum, the Mulberry Bend. Here the well-dressed families and closed shops—one with a sign in Hebrew —suggest that it is Saturday and that families are milling about after attending synagogue. Lazarus Levy—the proprietor of the shop at 30 East Broadway—was among twelve and a half pages of Levys listed in the 1898 city directory. He moved his business to East Houston Street within the year.

WHITNEY-PAGET WEDDING, NOVEMBER 12, 1895

THE BYRON COLLECTION. 93.1.1.17463

One of many high-profile Anglo-American weddings—considered an "epidemic" by *Munsey's Magazine*—to take place during the 1890s, the Whitney-Paget nuptials united the eldest daughter of financier and politician William Collins Whitney with the sixth son of the late Lord Alfred Henry Paget. Pauline Whitney and Almeric Hugh Paget exchanged vows in St. Thomas Church at Fifth Avenue and 53rd Street, the foremost place of worship, weddings, and funerals for those whose sumptuous residences lined this legendary stretch of Fifth Avenue. Luminaries at this celebration included President Grover Cleveland, under whom William Collins Whitney served as Secretary of the Navy.

SEVENTH AVE. AND WEST 30TH ST. — COLORED DISTRICT, 1903

THE BYRON COLLECTION, 93.1.1.18076

Byron took many photographs of this neighborhood, presumably on the same day, in what appears to be a concerted effort to document the community. In 1900 the African American population in all of New York's five boroughs was 2 percent of the total, or 60,666. Over 36,000 were living in Manhattan, concentrated in and around the neighborhood depicted here, centered on Seventh Avenue in the West 30s, and San Juan Hill, the area west of Columbus Circle, said to have been named in commemoration of the heroic efforts of African American veterans of the Spanish-American War. Both neighborhoods would be disrupted by major construction projects—the first by the mammoth Pennsylvania Station (1904–1910; see page 65) and the adjacent General Post Office (1913), the second by Lincoln Center for the Performing Arts (1962–1968) and the Lincoln Towers apartments (1962–1964).

WORTH ST. (EAST FROM #69), 1898

THE BYRON COLLECTION, 93.1.1.17165

This view of Worth Street, lined with horse carts and crates of goods, conveys two New York City phenomena. First is the lack of rear alleys in the city's grid in favor of more buildable square footage and thus more revenue for the money-driven metropolis, a bit of urban planning that causes streets and sidewalks clogged with delivery trucks to this day. Second is the proliferation of cast-iron warehouse buildings in this dry goods wholesale district, which allowed significant light to enter the deep buildings through large front windows, enabled by the narrow profile of the cast-iron columns.

WEST ST. LOOKING NORTH FROM CHARLES ST., c. 1899

THE BYRON COLLECTION, 93.1.1.17163

Oyster boats lined the Hudson River in this area near West Washington Market, the chief market for wholesale oysters. The oyster dealers stored and sold their stock from the houseboats, which were cooler than the indoor markets and, being mobile, streamlined the chore of bringing oysters to market. The Houseman family, whose boat is visible on the far left, had been in the business since 1810. By the 1930s the oyster boats were owned by the city and leased to dealers.

The apparently down-and-out man in the foreground could have been easily cropped from the frame, but Byron chose to include this bit of reality in his composition.

BLIZZARD OF 1899, 1899

THE BYRON COLLECTION. 93.1.1.171222

Beginning on Saturday evening, February 11, 1898, four days of nearly constant snow delivered over fourteen inches of fresh flakes atop an eight-inch base that had fallen a few days earlier. Although the Broadway cable cars and the elevated trains managed to operate throughout the blizzard, the city essentially came to a stop.

These day laborers, walking along the west colonnade of the *New York Herald* building at 34th Street and Broadway, were most likely hired by the Department of Street Cleaning to provide emergency help in clearing the city's streets. According to *The New Metropolis*, the going rate for such help was $2 per day; the City would incur expenses of $125,000 to $175,000 in dealing with a storm of this magnitude.

Byron took more than fifty photographs of the aftermath of the Blizzard of '99, but seems to have been frustrated by not being able to capture the storm itself (impossible because of the relatively long exposure time his camera required). This frustration is evidenced by several prints struck from negatives that were altered by the addition of spots to resemble falling snow.

**BLIZZARD OF 1899
(DUMPING SNOW IN THE EAST RIVER AT 38TH STREET), 1899**

THE BYRON COLLECTION, 93.1.1.14285

Even today, in cases of extreme snow accumulation, the Department of Sanitation, with the permission of the Department of Environmental Protection, dumps snow cleared from the streets into the city's rivers.

The monolithic Kip's Bay Brewing Company building, visible in the distance, still stands. It is now home to a variety of businesses and organizations as well as loft apartments, more germane to New York's now-prevalent professional and service industries than to the heavy industries that once lined its rivers.

PLAYING ON STREETS, 1908

This print falls under a Byron category called "Brooklyn, bad paving" and was probably commissioned by a group interested in improving the condition of these pot-holed streets. The fortunate side effect is this candid depiction of men and boys gathered on a Brooklyn street corner.

LITTLE ITALY, 1898

THE BYRON COLLECTION, 93.1.1.3170

Published in *The New Metropolis*, this image was commissioned to illustrate the chapter entitled "Child Life." Little Italy on Manhattan's Lower East Side was bounded by Houston Street on the north, Canal Street on the south, and Broadway and Mulberry Street to the west and east. Italian immigrants first settled here in the 1850s and quickly divided into Italian subgroups—Genoans, Calabrians, Sicilians, and Neapolitans settled in different areas from the Tuscans and Piedmontese. By the 1950s many of the Italian residents had moved to other boroughs or the suburbs, and the growing population of Chinatown began to expand into Little Italy, a trend that continues to this day.

BROADWAY AND CANAL ST., 1898

THE BYRON COLLECTION. 93.1.1.15216

This busy scene shows the intersection of Broadway and Canal Street in the year of the creation of Greater New York, the consolidation of the municipalities that now make up New York City's five boroughs. At the time Canal Street was the dividing line between Broadway's retail businesses to the south and wholesalers to the north.

STATEN ISLAND FERRY, WHITEHALL ST., 1901–1902

THE BYRON COLLECTION, 93.1.1.4161

In 1900 Staten Island had a population of 67,021 people; nearly 10,000 made the daily commute to Manhattan's Whitehall Street ferry terminal. In 1990 approximately 70,000 of 378,977 Staten Islanders followed suit. Today the picturesque journey from the Battery to St. George, Staten Island—free since 1997—is one of the city's great amenities, enjoyed by tourists and residents alike.

CROWD IN FRONT OF U.S. TREASURY, "SAVE FOOD" CAMPAIGN, 1919

In 1918 the United States Food Administration published the pamphlet *10 Lessons in Food Conservation*, which emphasized saving food as vital to winning World War I and focused on the importance of rebuilding the country's depleted supplies. The "Save Food" campaign depicted here is surely related to these efforts of the Food Administration.

Built as the U.S. Custom House on the site of the original Federal Hall, this Greek Revival masterpiece (1833–1842) by architects Town & Davis later became the U.S. Sub-Treasury Building, and is now Federal Hall National Memorial. John Quincy Adams Ward's 1883 statue of George Washington commemorates the spot where the first president took his oath of office. At the corner of Wall and Broad streets, the building occupies one of the most historic and valuable sites in New York City.

SAKS & COMPANY'S DISPLAY OF MODEL OF S.S. GIULIO CESARE, 1922

THE BYRON COLLECTION, 93.1.1.15408

This bird's-eye view of pedestrians crowding Saks's windows was taken from the "El" platform of the Sixth Avenue elevated railroad. A commission by the Italia America Line brought Byron to this site to document the attention garnered by a scale model of the Line's *Giulio Cesare* placed in the department store's popular Herald Square show windows during the ship's maiden voyage. The *Giulio Cesare* capsized and sank at Trieste in May 1945.

Saks opened at this location in 1902; it moved to its famous Fifth Avenue location in 1924.

BROADWAY AT WEST 79TH ST., 1914

THE BYRON COLLECTION. 93.1.1.17943

The advertisements atop the Oliver & Olson department store at Broadway and West 79th Street speak for themselves—and nearly double the height of the building. Yet another row of advertisements can be seen beyond, through the steel supports for the billboard. The building remains, without its advertising appendage, and now houses Filene's Basement, a discount clothing retailer with display widows reminiscent of those in this photograph.

JOHN LANZ, N.E. CORNER SEVENTH AVE. & 47TH ST., 1926

Commissioned by the New York Association for the Blind, Byron documented New York's blind and visually impaired community in more than 160 photographs, including eight personalized images of newsstand operators, like John Lanz, in all areas of the city.

The proliferation of blind vendors in major American cities resulted from 1899 legislation authorizing mayors of large cities to issue free licenses for blind adult citizens to sell goods and newspapers and to play instruments on the street.

BROADWAY, WEST SIDE NORTH FROM 155TH ST., 1922

Here Percy Byron has transcended his usual role of documentarian and risen to that of creative artist. This photomontage consists of a base-image of the barren Audubon Terrace complex at Broadway between 155th and 156th Streets, supplemented with street life—and even an airplane—cut and pasted from other photographs. The photographic assemblage was then re-photographed so that a clean print could be produced, probably for promotional purposes. While this montage is not the only example of "trick" photography by the Byron Company, it is the most extreme.

The bulk of this complex of museums and cultural institutions—including the Hispanic Society of America, the American Numismatic Society, the American Geographical Society, and the Museum of the American Indian—was constructed between 1904 and 1922. It was built on the former estate of, and named after, artist and naturalist John James Audubon. The challenge Byron faced in enlivening this scene has not changed over the years. The 1988 *AIA Guide to New York City* describes the site as "a cul-de-sac with no ground-floor activity (restaurants, shops, people, or movement), it has become an unused…backwater."

AT WORK

*As a great emporium of commerce,
growing in size and importance, New York
offers employment in a variety of pursuits to
the skillful, the steady, and the industrious.*

WILLIAM CHAMBERS

THINGS AS THEY ARE IN AMERICA, 1853

Over the years Byron captured New Yorkers in a wide range of employment situations. Images of people working in service industries—hotels, restaurants, and retail establishments—predominate. It is likely that these images were used for publicity, sales, and marketing purposes and for internal publications such as annual reports. Occasionally Byron composed group portraits of workers, but the vast majority of images were styled to show people actively working, and the often self-conscious appearance of his subjects implies that the photographs were anything but candid. This formality is to be expected, considering the long exposure times and the likelihood of Byron's using flashlight photography.

A large number of images document the role of industry in New York, reflecting the visceral toil of the New York wage earner. Others less explicitly include people at work, such as a street scene showing bill posters (page 59) or a new subway station with a motorman visible (page 62).

NEW YORK TELEPHONE COMPANY EXCHANGES, 1896

THE BYRON COLLECTION, 93.1.1.15998

The busy exchange at 18 Cortlandt Street, one of twelve operated by the New York Telephone Company at this time, had the most experienced operators staffing its 250-foot-long switchboard. Referred to as "Hello Girls" in a Byron-illustrated article in the March 1902 *Metropolitan Magazine,* telephone operators performing this skilled job of great value to both the company and subscribers were considered superior in the ranks of working women.

A New York Telephone Company pamphlet titled *An Ideal Occupation for Young Women* (c. 1910) promoted the work of the telephone operator as "an enjoyable public service" compared to the "soulless" work of a factory. It sought to recruit "normal young American women between the ages of 16–25," describing the ideal candidate as having "no pronounced impediment or foreign accents in her speech."

**CAROLYN LAUNDRY, 111 EAST 128TH ST.,
LINE OF LAUNDRY WAGONS, 1929**

THE BYRON COLLECTION, 93.1.1.6831

Byron documented the Carolyn Laundry inside and out. There are images of office interiors, laundry being processed, the mangle, and even the staff's theatrical production at their 1929 Christmas party. The range of prints shows a highly organized business as exemplified by this regiment of wagons. At the same time, Byron took a similar photograph of a row of motor-driven laundry trucks, suggesting that the transition to a fully motorized fleet was underway.

THOMAS A. EDISON, 1904

Between 1904 and 1907 Byron made portraits of Thomas Alva Edison (1847–1931) alone, with his first and later his second wife, with his son at the piano, at home, and in his New Jersey laboratory. Byron also photographed Edison's New York showroom, his phonographs, and his Kinetoscope, which provided the means for the first public showing of a motion picture in the United States, at New York's Koster and Bial's Music Hall in 1896.

Joseph Byron and Edison probably had much to talk about. Byron also was a great inventor, designing and building specialized cameras and lenses to accommodate the wide range of his photographic commissions and interests.

SERGEANT DUNN (WEATHER FORECASTER) & STAFF, 1895

The growth of skyscrapers in the vicinity of their long-time facility at 120 Broadway forced Sergeant Dunn and his staff to relocate to this four-story tower station at the tip of the Manhattan Life Building—then the tallest in the United States—at 66 Broadway, where their sensitive weather-predicting instruments could work without interference. Dunn (standing), a native Brooklynite, left his post in 1898 after fifteen years with the New York station of the United States Weather Bureau.

Previously a division of the military, the United States Weather Bureau was established in 1869 and transferred to the Department of Agriculture in 1891. The chief forecaster (Sergeant Dunn in this case) was referred to as the weather prophet.

BLACKWELL'S ISLAND FOR CONSUMPTIVES, 1903

THE BYRON COLLECTION, 93.1.1.4950

Blackwell's Island—a one-and-a-half-mile-long strip of land in the East River purchased by New York City in 1828 for $50,000—was home to several institutions for the down-and-out. In addition to the facility for consumptives (tuberculosis sufferers) depicted here, the island housed a penitentiary, an almshouse, an insane asylum, and other similar institutions, all built by convict labor. Previously known as Hog Island, the strip of land took on the name of the family that lived there for many years prior to its purchase by the City. In 1921 the island was renamed Welfare Island for its glut of social service institutions. That name held until the 1970s when New York State began to transform the island into a residential community to be called Roosevelt Island, today a relatively sleepy neighborhood with a population of just over 8,000.

MRS. ROBINSON'S BEAUTY PARLOR, 1915

THE BYRON COLLECTION, 93.1.1.10837

The first two decades of the twentieth century saw the mainstream popularization of hair straightening among African American women. Manufacturers began to respond to the demand and created products to help people straighten their hair and then shape it into waves. Opposition to this trend—criticizing the desire by black women to emulate white trends—did not seem to stem its popularity. The Byron Company photographed several rooms in Mrs. Robinson's extensive salon, including a wigmaking room, a spacious reception room, and a bedroom, probably the proprietor's. From the exterior, the salon was a nondescript residential four-story red brick building.

CHEF LEONI EXERCISING HIS COOKS ATOP THE HOTEL COMMODORE, 1920

THE BYRON COLLECTION, 93.1.1.6074

This is one in a series of photographs documenting Chef Leoni and his extensive staff and facilities at the recently completed Hotel Commodore (see page 64). Staff exercise sessions such as that depicted here were not uncommon. Byron also photographed the Siegel-Cooper sales clerks exercising atop the roof of the famous department store.

DELMONICO'S, CONFECTIONERY DEPARTMENT, 1902

THE BYRON COLLECTION, 93.1.1.6150

In addition to documenting the public face of New York's many institutions, Byron was expert at—and perhaps more committed to—capturing life behind the scenes. The skillful artistry of these confectioners, which could be taken for granted in another context, is clearly conveyed here. Byron photographed hundreds of restaurants and hotels over the years and usually included many aspects of the workforce in action.

Delmonico's, one of New York's finest establishments at the time, began at William Street in 1837 and followed society uptown, with a total of ten locations; this one was at Fifth Avenue and 44th Street. The original William Street location was re-opened as a new incarnation of Delmonico's Restaurant in 1998.

EDWARD BRANDUS, DEALER IN PAINTINGS, 1905

THE BYRON COLLECTION, 93.1.1.1700

Byron documented the home of art dealer Edward Brandus (1857–1939) in 1902. In 1905 he took a series of photographs of Brandus's works for sale, as seen here, probably while on view at J. P. Silo's Fifth Avenue Art Galleries (366 Fifth Avenue) prior to their 1906 auction at the Waldorf-Astoria Hotel, which brought $227,355.

BILL POSTERS, 1904

THE BYRON COLLECTION, 93.1.1.1666

Posting bills is a longstanding and controversial New York tradition. As early as the 1840s proprietors such as P. T. Barnum promoted circuses and theaters using banners and woodcut prints. Billboards naturally followed and increased with the development of roads, streetcars, and elevated lines. The advent of chromolithography in the 1880s led to larger and more colorful advertisements. The scale and profusion of such advertising resulted in public outcry against what many saw as an eyesore. Throughout the twentieth century, outdoor advertising has been both a bone of contention for New Yorkers and an essential icon of the city. Despite much regulation in the use of outdoor advertising, the controversy continues.

WARREN-NASH MOTOR CORP., GREASING SHACKLES AND HINGES, 1928

THE BYRON COLLECTION, 93.1.1.461

Percy Byron had been photographing Warren-Nash showrooms and automobiles for several years prior to this 1928 photograph. This image, taken at Warren-Nash's 131st Street and Broadway location, was probably used to promote the production of the 100,000th "Auto 400 Series," a landmark in the company's history.

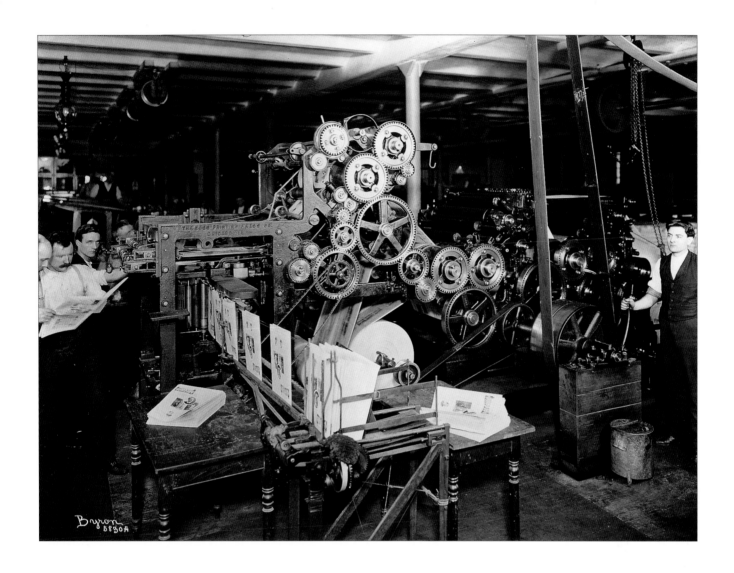

CHRISTIAN HERALD PRESS ROOM, 1898–1899

THE BYRON COLLECTION, 93.1.1.3182

First issued in New York in 1878, the *Christian Herald* was a leading religious magazine and charitable organization until financial hardship forced its demise in 1992. At the time of this photograph, the *Herald* was edited by Louis Klopsch. Its offices were at Bible House, the headquarters of the American Bible Society, at Astor Place; its press rooms and bindery were located nearby at the De Vinne Building.

This is one of several presses documented "in action" by the Byron Company over the years, including those of *Success Magazine*, *The Dramatic Mirror*, *the International Magazine Company*, and *McCall's Magazine*.

SUBWAY, HUDSON TUBES, c. 1908

Established by the Hudson and Manhattan Railroad, this rail line under the Hudson River opened on February 25, 1908, near the time of this photograph. Initially it ran only from Hoboken, New Jersey, to 19th Street in Manhattan but later expanded to link Newark, New Jersey, and lower Manhattan as well. The Hudson and Manhattan Railroad declared bankruptcy in 1954, and in 1962 the Port Authority Trans-Hudson (PATH) Corporation was formed to operate the system.

The station depicted here still exists. In 1976 the American Society of Civil Engineers declared the Hudson and Manhattan Railroad tunnels a National Historic Civil Engineering Landmark.

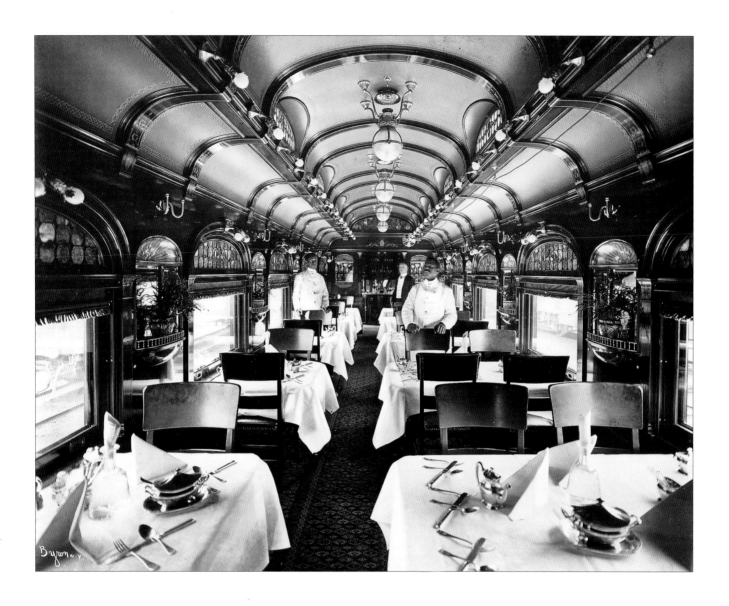

ERIE RAILROAD DINING CAR, 1902

THE BYRON COLLECTION, 93.1.1.4074

Completed in 1851, the Erie was the first railroad to use American-made iron rails and to direct train operations by telegraph. Along with these impressive pioneering credits, the Erie became known as "The Scarlet Woman of Wall Street" when her board of trustees rigged the railroad's stock value and embezzled the dividends. In 1893 the railroad owned or leased 800 locomotives, 450 passenger cars, and 42,000 freight cars. It traveled to hundreds of destinations, including Buffalo, Chicago, and Pittsburgh. There were five daily westbound trains from New York, three of which ended in Chicago, which was 999 miles away, with 108 stations en route. The journey took a night and two days.

HOTEL COMMODORE — VICE PRES. GEORGE W. SWEENY IN BUCKET, 1917

THE BYRON COLLECTION, 93.1.1.6053

The mammoth Hotel Commodore (Warren & Wetmore, architects), completed in 1919, had 1,956 guest rooms on 28 floors. The hotel at 42nd Street and Lexington Avenue claimed to have the largest banquet and ballroom in North America. It seated 3,500 and hosted many of the country's most important functions. In 1980 the glass-clad Grand Hyatt hotel opened, built over the structural shell of the Commodore.

This playful composition depicts the hotel's vice president, George W. Sweeny, and other hotel officials taking advantage of a photo opportunity as the structure neared completion.

PENNSYLVANIA DEPOT EXCAVATIONS, 1906

The construction of the monumental Pennsylvania Station required the demolition of 500 buildings and the digging of tunnels under the East and Hudson Rivers. Construction took more than fifteen years, but the result was a magnificent gateway to New York City, connecting Long Island and cities all along the Eastern Seaboard to the metropolis.

Outraged New Yorkers tried to stop the 1963 demolition of the masterpiece designed by architects McKim, Mead & White, but there were no legal grounds for interceding. The demolition of Pennsylvania Station galvanized the city's historic preservation movement, resulting in the 1965 formation of the New York Landmarks Preservation Commission.

NEW YORK CITY FIRE ENGINE NO. 72, 1915

THE BYRON COLLECTION, 93.1.1.17307

New York City Fire Engine No. 72 was established in 1900 at 22 East 12th Street in Manhattan, where it remained until it disbanded in 1916. Engine 72 was reorganized in 1917 at the same address, and in 1918 it joined forces with Engine 41. In 1972 Engine 72 was up and running again in the Bronx, where it remains an active precinct today.

Until the Uniformed Firefighters Association introduced split shifts in 1919, New York City firefighters were required to be on continuous duty, with time off for two meals daily and ten days of leave each year for regular firemen, fourteen for officers.

MOTOR CORPS OF AMERICA, 1920

Part of the National League for Women's Services, the Motor Corps of America was approved by the United States Army to help with wounded soldiers who had returned from war. A *New York Times* article of January 19, 1919, reported that the National League for Women's Services had been organizing entertainment for soldiers from Fox Hills Hospital, the country's largest army hospital, on Staten Island. The Motor Corps of America escorted the soldiers to the entertainment—an amateur boxing match judged by society women.

NEW YORK CITY DEPARTMENT OF PUBLIC CHARITIES, 1902

THE BYRON COLLECTION, 93.1.1.17252

The Department of Public Charities was formed as an independent entity in 1895 when its former parent organization, the Department of Charities and Correction, was abolished. The department governed all city-owned charitable institutions, hospitals, places of detention, and the public cemetery.

MAYOR MCCLELLAN, 1904

THE BYRON COLLECTION, 93.1.1.9069

Byron must have pleased his client—*Success Magazine*—with this image, portraying a confident Mayor George B. McClellan (1865–1940) not long after his defeat of incumbent Seth Low. McClellan served two terms as a respected and competent leader of the city before abandoning politics to write and teach at Princeton University.

The newspaper headline visible in the photograph refers to the Japanese-Russian war in Manchuria, where armored battleships, self-propelled torpedoes, and land mines were first used.

FLAG FACTORY — MAKING UNITED STATES FLAGS, 1913

THE BYRON COLLECTION, 93.1.1.4229

This patriotic scene provides insufficient leads for fruitful investigation. While the calendars lining the far wall establish the year of this photograph, their mastheads all bear the company name "Royal"—which does not appear in New York City directories at that time, suggesting that either the calendars are not from the company depicted or that this scene is not in New York.

E. R. DURKEE & CO., ELMHURST, L.I., SALAD DRESSING MACHINE, 1927

THE BYRON COLLECTION, 93.1.1.4120

Eugene R. Durkee founded his company in 1851, and by 1857 his original "secret recipe" dressing for salads and meats had won numerous awards for excellence. The company went on to create sauces and gravy mixes, to import olives, and to package and sell shredded coconut. In 1906 the government turned to E. W. Durkee (Eugene's son) to write federal standards for spices and extracts. This factory at Elmhurst, Long Island (Queens), joined the existing Brooklyn plant in 1917. Durkee's reputation for being a good employer is evident in the several years of documentation by Byron Company photographs, which include playful group portraits, gardens on the factory grounds, and staff dining rooms. Durkee Famous Foods was absorbed by the Glidden Company in 1980 and then transferred to the Consumer Products Division of the SCM Corporation.

KABO CORSET CO., 1915

The Chicago-based Kabo Corset Company had its New York offices at 800 Sixth Avenue near West 45th Street. In Bowman's *Corset and Brassiere Trade* directory of 1920, Kabo was listed as "Manufacturers of back lace, front lace, maternity and sport corsets, also corset waists, brassieres, all types, garters and sanitary specialties." Byron's photographs were most likely commissioned to illustrate a promotional piece.

AMERICAN ENKA CORP. SHOWROOM, 1938

THE BYRON COLLECTION. 93.1.1.179

The renowned advertising firm of J. Walter Thompson Company commissioned this photograph for the American Enka Corporation, manufacturers of rayon and rayon fabrics. In 1938, on the eve of the 1939 New York World's Fair with its "world of tomorrow" theme, synthetic materials were gaining tremendous popularity and acceptance. Rayon was invented in 1884 but was not commonly used in fashion until the 1930s. This photograph is a compelling marriage of two of New York's great industries—the Madison Avenue advertising world and Seventh Avenue's glamorous fashion industry. The May 15, 1938, issue of Vogue was replete with advertisements for rayon manufacturers, including a two-page spread by American Enka. Titled *Fashion Approval in Floria Sheer of Enka Rayon*, the ad extols the use of Enka's floria sheer rayon fabric by Lady In White fashions.

The 1937 Yellow Pages list American Enka—one of 101 entries under "Rayon"—at 271 Church Street.

Though one can dine in New York, one could not dwell there.

OSCAR WILDE, 1887

On the island of Manhattan the people may be divided into seven classes:
the very rich, the rich, the prosperous, the well-to-do comfortable,
the well-to-do uncomfortable, the comfortable or contented poor,
and the submerged or uncomfortable poor.

E. IDELL ZEISLOFT, THE NEW METROPOLIS, 1899

*I*dell Zeisloft's authoritative description of Manhattan's population, while perhaps overstated, is in accord with the wide range of living conditions documented by the Byron Company and other photographers at the turn of the century. While Byron did find his way into the homes of the less fortunate, he did not share the mission of social reform that inspired his contemporary, Jacob Riis, to document the squalid conditions of tenement life. The wealthy—and the popular press that provided a glimpse of their conspicuous consumption to the eager public—were Byron's inspiration. Joseph Byron's 1894 commission from publisher P. F. Collier to photograph the homes of New York's Four Hundred to be featured in *Once A Week,* led to a long string of commissions from social climbers hoping to find their homes gracing the pages of this popular weekly as well.

Byron also garnered commissions to photograph the homes of many of the actors and actresses whom he had repeatedly photographed on stage. This work often reveals a personal connection between the photographer and his subject, with images of the residents at ease in their homes—a relationship that seems not to have existed with his wealthiest clients, who are conspicuously absent from Byron's portraits of their homes.

Other commissions led Byron to less traditional homes, such as Sailors' Snug Harbor (page 86) and the Kings County Almshouse (page 88), which have become a wonderful document of what "home" might have been to less fortunate New Yorkers. As holds true through the spectrum of the Byron Company's work, the post-World War I images tend to reflect a more specialized commercial clientele, resulting in commissions such as the apartment houses depicted on pages 96 and 97.

RESIDENCE OF F. BERKLEY SMITH, 1904

Son of author Frances Hopkinson Smith, F. Berkley Smith (1868–1931) resided and worked at this charming Gothic Revival row house near Gramercy Park, at 129 East 19th Street. Smith was an architect and practiced that profession until 1896, when he turned his attention to painting. Built originally as a stable in 1860–1861, the house still stands today, under landmark protection.

MRS. LESLIE CARTER, 1905

THE BYRON COLLECTION, 93.1.1.8664

Of the several photographs Byron took of the home of Leslie Carter (1862–1937), only this one included the fiery redheaded actress in person. She sits on the right, studying a crystal ball with a friend. This was the year of Carter's most praised role, as the tragic heroine of *Adrea*, in an otherwise mediocre acting career. Byron photographed the 1905 production; his documentation of Carter's home was probably in response to popular demand for information about the star's personal life.

SLUM INTERIOR, 1896

THE BYRON COLLECTION. 93.1.1.17888

Byron made a few exposures of the tenement home and workshop where artificial flowers were assembled by this immigrant family. Percy Byron accompanied his father on this assignment for St. John's Guild Floating Hospital and recalled much later that it was taken in the "East Side Slum Section," or the Lower East Side. Here Byron clearly joins the tradition of documenting the ills of tenement life established by the social reformer Jacob Riis.

Despite the harsh reality of this situation, Byron was able to capture a level of humanity conspicuously absent in his extensive documentation of the homes of New York's wealthiest citizens.

INTERIOR — LILLIAN RUSSELL'S HOME, 1904

THE BYRON COLLECTION, 93.1.1.9201

Channing Pollock, the press agent for the Shuberts, with whom Lillian Russell was under contract, released a story in the fall of 1904 about her new home at 161 West 57th Street, complete with flashlight photographs by Byron. The home is described in Parker Morell's 1940 biography of Russell, *Lillian Russell, the Era of Plush:*

> There was a Louis Sixteenth music room, a Marie Antoinette drawing room, an Old
> English supper room, a Dutch dining room, a Turkish den with the inevitable Cozy
> Corner done in proper Duveen style [depicted here], and an old-fashioned pink-
> and-gold American bedroom, with an enormous brass double bedstead and a tiled
> bathroom showing plainly a sturdy but undoubtedly telltale weighing scale.

In 1907 as her acting career required more work on the road, Russell decided to auction her belongings and sell the house. The three-day sale of furnishings brought a mere $74,274, a fraction of her initial investment.

MRS. WILLIAM ASTOR RESIDENCE, 1894

THE BYRON COLLECTION, 93.1.1.9668

Despite her husband's 1892 death, Caroline Webster Schermerhorn Astor—New York's premier socialite of the Gilded Age—continued with plans to build a hotel on the site of this Fifth Avenue and 34th Street palace. The hotel would merge with the adjacent Waldorf Hotel, completed in 1893 by her nephew William Waldorf Astor, to become the Waldorf-Astoria. Mrs. Astor and her son, John Jacob Astor IV, built a new home (1891–1895) on the northeast corner of Fifth Avenue and 65th Street, and in 1929 the Waldorf-Astoria Hotel was demolished to make way for the construction of the Empire State Building. The hotel's refined Art Deco successor soon rose on Park Avenue between 49th and 50th Streets.

JOHN JACOB ASTOR RESIDENCE, 1897

THE BYRON COLLECTION, 93.1.1.18060

Caroline Webster Schermerhorn Astor and her son John Jacob Astor IV commissioned architect Richard Morris Hunt to build this double house (1891–1895) on the northeast corner of Fifth Avenue and 65th Street. Their new home was necessitated by the demolition of their previous residence at Fifth Avenue and 34th Street to make way for their Hotel Astor, which later merged with the adjacent Waldorf to become the renowned Waldorf–Astoria.

WILLIAM COLLINS WHITNEY RESIDENCE, 1901–1902

THE BYRON COLLECTION, 93.1.1.17186

William Collins Whitney and his second wife were the third owners of this mansard-roofed brownstone mansion. Mrs. Whitney died just prior to the 1899 completion of its three-year interior renovation, and her husband died in 1904 of appendicitis. Built by architect William Schickel in the early 1880s, the house passed through several hands over the years, until its 1942 demolition, just nine months after the death of its final occupant, Gertrude Vanderbilt Whitney.

W. C. WHITNEY, DRAWING ROOM, 1899–1900

William Collins Whitney spent more than $1,000,000 renovating the Fifth Avenue and 68th Street home that he shared with his second wife. Under the mastery of renowned architect Stanford White, this 1896-to-1899 project resulted in one of New York's most sumptuous Gilded Age interiors.

T. A. HAVEMEYER RESIDENCE, 1898

THE BYRON COLLECTION, 93.1.1.17150

First occupied by the Theodore A. Havemeyer family in 1867–1868, this mansard-roofed mansion on the south-west corner of Madison Avenue and 38th Street was remodeled by society architect Richard Morris Hunt in 1891–1892. Seven Byron photographs were featured in a 1895 *Once A Week* article about Mrs. Havemeyer and her grand home. This photograph was taken the year after Theodore Havemeyer's 1897 death. Havemeyer and his brother made their fortune in sugar refining, and during the 1890s controlled as much as 98 percent of the U. S. sugar industry.

Henry Osborne Havemeyer was the president of the family's sugar refining business until his death in 1907. Designed by Charles C. Haight, the architect of the similarly turreted New York Cancer Hospital which still stands at 106th Street and Central Park West, the Havemeyer mansion was built between 1890 and 1891 on the northeast corner of Fifth Avenue and 66th Street. The home was best known for its sumptuous interior decoration by Louis Comfort Tiffany and Samuel Colman, commissioned by Havemeyer and his wife Louisine in 1890. The interior design provided a distinctive setting for the Havemeyers' collection of Impressionist and Old Master paintings.

ANDREW CARNEGIE RESIDENCE, FIFTH AVE. & 91ST STREET, c. 1905

Designed by architects Babb, Cook & Willard (built 1899–1903), this Georgian- and Renaissance-inspired château was sited far uptown at Fifth Avenue and 91st Street so that steel magnate Andrew Carnegie and his wife Louise could have a spacious garden. The free-standing mansion was occupied by the family until Louise's death in 1946. It then served as the Columbia School of Social Work until acquired by the Smithsonian Institution in 1972 to house the Cooper-Hewitt National Design Museum. The museum is founded upon collections originally assembled by the Cooper and Hewitt families for the Cooper Union for the Advancement of Science and Art.

SAILORS' SNUG HARBOR — CHURCH AND MUSIC HALL, 1899

THE BYRON COLLECTION, 93.1.1.14146

Established by the 1801 will of Captain Robert Richard Randall, who bequeathed his fortune to the establishment and maintenance of a "home for aged, decrepit, and worn-out" American sailors, Sailors' Snug Harbor opened its New Brighton, Staten Island, site in 1833 with twenty sailors. After losing a lengthy battle against the landmarking of the historic buildings, the Sailors' Snug Harbor trustees moved the institution to the North Carolina coast in the 1970s. Purchased by New York City and dubbed the Snug Harbor Cultural Center, the buildings and site now accommodate more than seventy organizations, including a botanical garden and children's museum.

ELBRIDGE T. GERRY RESIDENCE, 1899–1900

Designed by renowned architect Richard Morris Hunt, the Elbridge Thomas Gerry residence (1891–1894) on the southeast corner of Fifth Avenue and 61st Street was built for Gerry and his family. Gerry, a prominent lawyer and philanthropist, eventually gave up his law practice to devote his time to the New York Society for the Prevention of Cruelty to Children, a charity he helped establish in 1874. The house was demolished in 1927, the year of Gerry's death, and replaced by the Pierre Hotel, completed in 1930.

KINGS COUNTY ALMSHOUSE, 1900

Maintained by the Department of Charities and Corrections of Kings County (Brooklyn), this almshouse shared a sixty-five-acre site with the Kings County Hospital and the Long Island Hospital for the Insane. While the grounds were beautifully laid out, the facilities were notoriously overcrowded and shabby. The women's almshouse was established in 1850, and a men's section was added in 1869.

MRS. ELLIOTT RESIDENCE, 1902

THE BYRON COLLECTION, 93.1.1.9915

Byron produced thirty interior views of this residence belonging to an elusive Mrs. Elliott. The Byron Company left no further information about her, and attempts to identify her have been unsuccessful.

ELSIE DE WOLFE, 1896

THE BYRON COLLECTION, 93.1.1.18271

Just two blocks away from F. Berkley Smith's home and studio, socialite and decorator Elsie de Wolfe shared the charming house at 122 East 17th Street with her friend Elisabeth Marbury from 1887 to 1911. She explored her interior decorating ideas here, before her first significant commission—Stanford White's Colony Club—in 1905 and the 1913 publication of her treatise *The House in Good Taste*.

TIFFANY HOUSE, c. 1900

THE BYRON COLLECTION, 93.1.1.18259

King's Handbook of New York (1893) described the Tiffany House as "one of the most unique and attractive dwelling houses in America." Commissioned by Tiffany & Company founder Charles Lewis Tiffany, the house was designed by Stanford White in conjunction with Tiffany's artist son, Lewis Comfort, who was responsible for the unusual roof design and the interior decoration of the house. The structure, built from 1883 to 1885, actually included three separate residences, one or more of which was occupied by Tiffany family members until Louis Comfort Tiffany's death in 1933, three years prior to the building's demolition.

ISAAC V. BROKAW RESIDENCE, 1901–1902

THE BYRON COLLECTION, 93.1.1.17192

Clothing manufacturer Isaac V. Brokaw built his French Renaissance mansion on the northeast corner of Fifth Avenue and 79th Street. Designed by the architectural firm of Rose and Stone, the residence was completed in 1899. During the ensuing years, Brokaw built homes for two sons and a daughter on adjacent lots, establishing a Brokaw stronghold at this intersection. The Brokaw residences were demolished in the 1960s, making way for an apartment building.

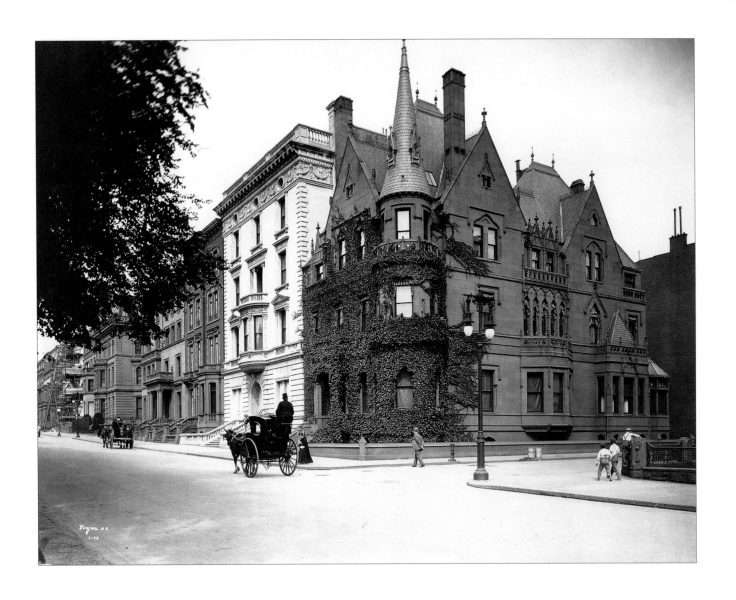

GEORGE GOULD RESIDENCE, 1901–1902

THE BYRON COLLECTION, 93.1.1.17185

George Gould and his wife, former actress Edith Kingdon, built this 50-room mansion on the northeast corner of Fifth Avenue and 67th Street after inheriting a railroad and telegraph empire from George's father, Jay Gould, in 1892. To keep up with the style and social demands of the times, the Goulds demolished their château and replaced it with a Renaissance-style mansion in 1906.

JOSIAH M. FISKE RESIDENCE, 1901–1902

The Gothic-inspired home on the southeast corner of Fifth Avenue and 70th Street was that of stockbroker Josiah Fiske and his wife, Martha. John Sloane, partner in the very successful firm of carpet and furniture retailers, W. & J. Sloane, occupied the residence directly adjacent, at 883 Fifth Avenue.

W. H. VANDERBILT RESIDENCES (TWIN HOUSES), 1898

THE BYRON COLLECTION. 93.1.1.17179

William H. Vanderbilt purchased the entire blockfront on the west side of Fifth Avenue between 51st and 52nd streets in 1879, having recently inherited a fortune from his father, Cornelius Vanderbilt. Architects John B. Snook and Charles Atwood designed twin houses connected by a glass atrium and entrance vestibule, and the famed Herter Brothers decorated the houses with such extravagance that *Artistic Houses* devoted 17 pages to its interiors upon their completion in 1883. W. H. Vanderbilt and his wife lived in the southern house, while their two daughters and sons-in-law occupied the other.

250 RIVERSIDE DRIVE & 315 WEST 97TH STREET, N.Y.C., 1939

THE BYRON COLLECTION, 93.1.1.16762

The Byron Company's residential commissions in the 1920s and 1930s were not nearly as glamorous as photographing the homes of New York's Four Hundred at the turn of the century. These apartment house commissions were more typical of commercial photography of the day and often lacked personal attachment. The Sutton Place Apartments photograph (facing page), for instance, was commissioned by Kohler, the plumbing fixture manufacturer.

SUTTON PLACE APARTMENTS, 57TH ST., N.Y., 1926

THE BYRON COLLECTION, 93.1.1.16747

CORNELIUS VANDERBILT RESIDENCE, 1920

THE BYRON COLLECTION, 93.1.1.10529

The home of Cornelius Vanderbilt II and his wife, Alice Gwynne, was the largest of the several Vanderbilt family residences that dotted Fifth Avenue. The imposing French Château–style mansion was one of only three houses on Fifth Avenue to take up an entire block-front (the other two were the Carnegie and Frick residences). Originally built in 1879–1883, the house was enlarged and redesigned just ten years later by architect George B. Post in consultation with his former teacher, Richard Morris Hunt. Its grand facades graced Fifth Avenue between 57th and 58th streets, and the length of Grand Army Plaza along 58th Street. No less fashionable than the mansion it replaced, the Bergdorf Goodman department store was erected on this site in 1928.

AT PLAY

*In this Paris of the New World, the tendency is to social life,
to fraternal union, to manifold forms of confederation. There is
little opportunity here for ascetic seclusion, or for withdrawal from the
brightening attrition of humanity. There is also little inclination for
such separation. The air of the metropolis is full of mercurial
activities, and gregariousness becomes inevitable.*

MOSES KING

KING'S HANDBOOK OF NEW YORK CITY, 1893

From the social events of New York's elite to a day at the beach, the Byron Company captured the city's pastimes. However as the studio's work became increasingly specialized, particularly after World War I, the number of images that might fall into this category diminished.

Byron photographed no less than 100 "dinners," ranging from the most banal corporate banquets to such eccentric episodes as the C. K. G. Billings Horseback Dinner (page 111), at New York's most famous restaurants and banquet facilities. Company picnics and year-round outdoor leisure activities caught Byron's lens, as did the all-night fêtes of private clubs and exclusive cliques.

New York City, then as now, offered a tremendous variety of recreational opportunities for its citizenry, rich and poor. Manhattan's Central Park and the green spaces dotting all five boroughs were truly parks for the people, accessible and well appointed. Some of the world's finest restaurants and most exclusive private clubs catered to those needing society's approval. A strong rail network facilitated pleasure trips to the shore or the country, and eccentric services such as the Turkish Bath (page 112) and the Zander Institute (page 113) make today's oxygen bars and aromatherapy boutiques pale in comparison.

BATHING, MIDLAND BEACH (STATEN ISLAND), 1898

THE BYRON COLLECTION, 93.1.1.17470

Midland Beach—recently made accessible by rail at the time of Byron's visit—was one of a series of fashionable seasonal resort beaches along Staten Island's south shore. Water pollution and devastating fires saw the decline of this popular resort area after World War II. Today the beach is administered by the City of New York Parks and Recreation Department. The surrounding area is a year-round residential community.

CARLEY LIFE FLOAT CO., 1905

THE BYRON COLLECTION, 93.1.1.3092

The Carley Life Float Company probably commissioned the Byron Company—knowing the firm through its prolific steamship photography—to document this lively affair at the Battery. Although the details of the event are not known, it appears to be some sort of contest or race, presumably in promotion of the company's lifeboats. The Carley Life Float Company rented offices in the nearby Produce Exchange building, visible in the distance to the right, with the square tower.

SKATING, VAN CORTLANDT PARK, 1898

THE BYRON COLLECTION, 93.1.1.14409

The 1,132-acre Van Cortlandt Park was named for Jacobus Van Cortlandt, mayor of New York from 1710–1719, whose wife Eva was given the tract by her adoptive father. Van Cortlandt descendants held the Bronx property until 1899 when it was sold to the city after years of use as park land. The ever-popular winter sport of ice skating was easily accommodated on the park's lake.

SKATING, CENTRAL PARK, 1904

Skating on the lake in Central Park was enormously popular, as evidenced in this view of skaters at the famous Bow Bridge (designed by Calvert Vaux, 1860), with the fashionable apartments of Central Park West visible beyond. Unlike its counterpart at Van Cortlandt Park in the northern Bronx, Central Park's lake was entirely manmade.

THE CENTURY CLUB — GROUP COSTUMED, 1917

THE BYRON COLLECTION, 93.1.1.2626

Founded in 1846 to promote the advancement of art and literature, the Century Club membership was characterized in the 1893 edition of *King's Handbook of New York* as fun-loving "jesters" who had "a superb disregard for the money standard of value." This notorious frivolity was evidenced annually in an eccentric Twelfth Night celebration, a tradition that began in 1916 in celebration of the club's seventieth anniversary. In describing the event in *Century Association 1847–1946*, Henry F. Pringle wrote, "Taxicabs with hot-water bottles or ice packs, as the exigencies of the occasion may require, may be ordered for 3:30 a.m."

THE HYDE BALL, 1905

THE BYRON COLLECTION. 93.1.1.20197

A team of five from the Byron studio made 189 11×14-inch negatives between 8 p.m. on Tuesday January 31, 1905, and 6 a.m. the following morning. The John Hazen Hyde Ball, held at Sherry's on Fifth Avenue and 44th Street, was a costumed extravaganza with ballroom dancing and two suppers, culminating in a 7 a.m. breakfast for those who had survived the evening. Hyde, a twenty-eight-year-old Harvard graduate whose father had given him control of the family's Equitable Life Assurance Society of the United States, entertained his guests in a Versailles-inspired setting designed by architect Whitney Warren.

Depicted here, in one of many group portraits of the evening, are Mrs. Sydney Smith, Mr. Philip Clark, Mrs. James Burden, Stanford White, Mr. Harry T. Smith, Mr. J. Norman De R. Whitehouse, Mr. Sydney Smith, and Mrs. Stuyvesant Fish.

T. E. FITZGERALD BAR, 1912

THE BYRON COLLECTION, 93.1.1.17847

While the range of clientele seen here at T. E. Fitzgerald's bar at Sixth Avenue and West 44th Street suggests that social and economic barriers could be overcome by the need for midday refreshment (the clock indicates that it is just after noon), women and ethnic minorities are conspicuously absent from this place of leisure.

HOTEL WOODWARD — THE BAR, 1937

THE BYRON COLLECTION, 93.1.1.6816

Located at Broadway and West 55th Street, the Hotel Woodward was not one of New York's grand hotels, but this photograph suggests that it attracted a fashionable crowd to its sleek vaulted bar. It is likely that these patrons are actually models, styled to attract a certain clientele through advertising, not an unusual tactic at this point in Percy Byron's career. Byron photographed the Woodward on several occasions between 1917 and 1937, perhaps because the Byron studio, in two of its many locations (250 West 54th Street and 1695 Broadway), was just around the corner from this watering hole.

PICNIC AT NEWBURGH, N.Y., 1897

THE BYRON COLLECTION, 93.1.1.2800

Despite the oppressive attire of the day, these women picnicking in Newburgh seem to be enjoying a moment of unfettered play, posing with pipes and cigars. The event was an excursion up the Hudson on the *Bay Queen* by music publishers M. Witmark & Sons. Company employees left their West 28th Street headquarters for a day of pleasure on the Hudson River and in Newburgh.

DAUGHTERS OF THE AMERICAN REVOLUTION, 1898

THE BYRON COLLECTION, 93.1.1.18395

This archetypal image depicts the fledgling Daughters of the American Revolution—presumably the New York Chapter—just eight years after its founding. This photograph was featured in Zeisloft's *The New Metropolis* in the chapter entitled "Ye Old Inns & Modern Clubs."

INDIANS, 1913

THE BYRON COLLECTION, 93.1.1.4466

On the back of this print is written "Chiefs of the Redskins, original owners of the City, return to view their late hunting grounds from the roof of the highest hotel in the World, The McAlpin on Broadway." Byron photographed over thirty portraits of Native American men and women during this 1913 shoot at the Hotel McAlpin—perhaps an exploitive publicity stunt by the hotel.

C. K. G. BILLINGS HORSEBACK DINNER AT SHERRY'S, 1908

Since it was featured in Grace Mayer's *Once Upon a City,* this quintessential image has epitomized the societal decadence that was so often the subject of Byron's work. Equestrian fanatic and capitalist C. K. G. Billings invited 36 guests to dine on horseback with custom-made dining trays and waiters dressed as grooms at a hunting party, in an elaborately decorated Sherry's Restaurant. The event took place on the eve of the opening of Billings's new $200,000 stable at 196th Street and Fort Washington Road, in what is now Fort Tryon Park in upper Manhattan.

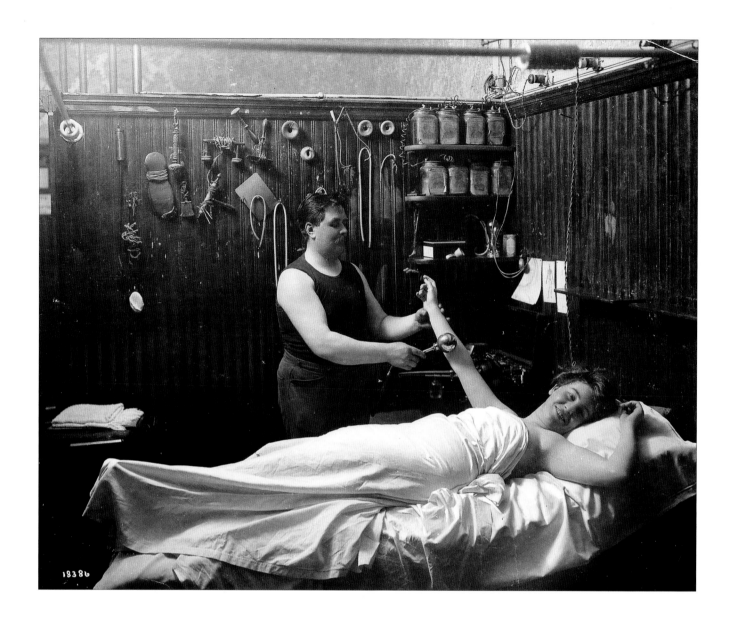

TURKISH BATH, REPOSING ROOM, 1904

THE BYRON COLLECTION, 93.1.1.16039

In interviewing Percy Byron about his father's series of photographs of a women's Turkish bath, *Once Upon a City* author Grace Mayer discovered that this speculative work was sold to the *New York Herald*, which published it in an exposé of the baths (three of which existed at the time) on November 6, 1904. The establishment depicted here, thought by Percy Byron to be in the East 70s near Lexington Avenue, put New York's well-to-do women through a strenuous ritual of wet and dry heat, swimming, massage, facials and manicures, hairdressing, luncheon with wine, and gossip.

ZANDER INSTITUTE, 1908

THE BYRON COLLECTION, 93.1.1.5293

Jonas Gustaf Wilhelm Zander (1835–1920) was a Swedish physician who invented a therapeutic method of exercise carried out by means of special apparatus such as that seen here. Zander began his work in the 1860s and established the Zander Institute in London, where he published *Mechanical Exercise: A Means of Cure* (1883) before coming to New York. His hope was that his equipment, which employed gradual muscle resistance, would supplement normal gymnasiums that excluded women, older people, and "weakly" people of either sex. The Zander Institute was located at 20 Central Park South.

DIRIGIBLE BALLOON RACE, BEECHY WINNER, 1908

This enchanting image was probably captured by Percy Byron during the second of his 11 years in Edmonton. Beechy in Saskatchewan was a quick trip from Edmonton on the Transcontinental Line, which also enabled these balloon barnstormers to move from town to town to show off their novel mode of transport. The rubber-sealed leather balloons were often taken to 1,000 feet, from which height passengers would parachute to the ground, adding to the drama and spectacle of the day. The first balloon flight in Saskatchewan was in Saskatoon in August 1908. This event at Beechy must have occurred shortly thereafter.

CITY KIDS

Young people in New York
have the same good time, on
slight provocation, that they
do elsewhere in the world.

JOHN C. VAN DYKE
THE NEW NEW YORK, 1909

Like no other subject, the inclusion of children in the camera's frame can transform an image of adversity into one of hope or even glee. In the following photographs, the realities of an orphanage, a derelict slum, and the tension of labor unrest are all somehow mitigated by the playfulness or innocence of children. Other images do not disguise so well. Depictions of children are replete throughout the Byron Collection, though usually as incidental subjects in other scenes of New York City life. Relatively few images explicitly document the children of the wealthy—perhaps an extension of the common belief that children were to be seen and not heard.

VIRGINIA DAY NURSERY, 1906

Founded in 1879, the Virginia Day Nursery cared for the children of working single mothers from the immigrant communities of the Lower East Side. This photograph was taken at the nursery's East Fifth Street location, built in 1901, and is one of several Byron images depicting the activities and handicrafts of the fortunate students. The photographs were most likely employed in fundraising and promotion for the institution. The Virginia Day Nursery remains active today at its East Tenth Street location, with 67 children of lower-income working or student parents, and a therapeutic program for children with special needs.

SAINT THOMAS, 1906

Saint Thomas Chapel, on 60th Street between Second and Third Avenues, was sustained by its wealthy Fifth Avenue cousin, St. Thomas Church. Behind the chapel, fronting 59th Street, was St. Thomas House, which was used for day care and teaching, and included a gymnasium, presumably the one depicted here. The parish conducted a cadet corps and drill team—which could explain the exercises in which these youngsters are engaged.

NEW YORK FOUNDLING HOSPITAL, 1899–1900

Founded in 1869 by the Sisters of Charity, the New York Foundling Hospital sought to alleviate the common nine-
teenth-century problem of abandoned babies, offspring of unwed mothers who were too ashamed and frightened
to tell their parents of their plight. From 1873 until 1958 when it moved to 1175 Third Avenue, the hospital was
located at 175 East 68th Street. Now occupying a modern facility at Sixth Avenue and 17th Street, the New York
Foundling Hospital is still operated by the Sisters of Charity, who no longer take in abandoned babies but instead
care for very sick infants from hospitals throughout the city.

ORPHAN ASYLUM, 73RD ST. AND RIVERSIDE DRIVE, 1899–1900

THE BYRON COLLECTION, 93.1.1.241

The oldest of its kind in the United States, the Orphan Asylum Society was founded in 1806, according to the 1893 *King's Handbook of New York*, to "minister to the wants of the parentless children of the community, and train them up in the paths of virtue." The Riverside Drive site was secured in 1835, and accommodated 250 children. Only children under age ten were admitted, and they were sent on to "Christian homes" when they reached age fourteen.

ARBOR DAY, TOMPKINS SQUARE, 1904

THE BYRON COLLECTION, 93.1.1.17806

Byron's composition of this charming group owes much of its success to the oddity of the teacher's domineering headpiece. Tompkins Square (not Thompson Square, as inscribed on the original negative), bordered by East Seventh and Tenth Streets and Avenues A and B, was not always as peaceful as this Arbor Day scene suggests—it has been the site of countless riots and demonstrations since the mid-nineteenth century, most recently around issues of homelessness.

Arbor Day, a quintessential American holiday to encourage the planting and care of trees, was first celebrated in Nebraska in 1872. Soon other states adopted the tradition, with the date of each state's celebration depending upon the best planting time for the area, from January in some southern states to May in the north. New York's Arbor Day is the last Friday in April.

HUDSON-BANK GYMNASIUM, 1898

The Outdoor Recreation League was founded in 1898 to provide for "proper and sufficient exercise and recreation places, playgrounds, and open air gymnasiums for the people." Byron captured the success of the Hudson-Bank Gymnasium, located within the new DeWitt Clinton Park between 11th and 12th Avenues and 52nd and 54th Streets, during its inaugural year in several photographs that document constructive play and exercise in this notoriously dangerous Hell's Kitchen neighborhood.

HARLEM SLUM AREA, 1932

THE BYRON COLLECTION, 93.1.3.38

These adventurous kids provided a wonderful Depression-era composition of summer in New York City. Based on Byron's title, this scene presumably took place in the Harlem River. Byron noted that this photograph was taken on June 11, 1932, and listed "Wesley MacArdell Films" on the original negative sleeve, though no other reference to this film company nor the purpose of this and twelve similar photographs has been found.

BROOKLYN STRIKE, 1899

THE BYRON COLLECTION, 93.1.1.1766

The 1899 Brooklyn Car Strike echoed its 1895 predecessor in that its main objective was to reduce the workday to ten hours. At the time, the Rapid Transit Company was in the process of absorbing the five boroughs' individual transit companies into one system. The Nassau Company (Brooklyn) was at the crux of the strike, which began on July 16 after several employees had been discharged for lack of discipline. Disruptive violence ensued against streetcars, elevated trains, motormen, and conductors, with supportive women and children taking part in the riots on the night of July 19. Perhaps the boys depicted here, apparently in trouble, took part. Policemen from Manhattan were called in to help control the uprisings, an interborough reallocation of resources made possible by the 1898 consolidation of Greater New York.

CHRISTIAN HERALD CHILDREN'S HOME, 1896–1898

THE BYRON COLLECTION, 93.1.1.3199

These youngsters—some captivated by Byron's camera—await fresh water at the *Christian Herald*'s Nyack summer camp. The children, mostly from Lower East Side immigrant families, would travel by boat up the Hudson River and then by carriage down Christian Herald Road to the camp, where they would enjoy ten days away from the city. Over the course of a summer, the camp would accommodate thousands of needy children between the ages of six and eleven. The Christian Herald Youth Program continues to operate its summer camp, although the children now spend two weeks at a time in rural Pennsylvania.

CHILDREN'S PARTY, 1904

THE BYRON COLLECTION, 93.1.1.3157

This children's costume party took place in the comfortable suburb of Mt. Vernon, New York, at the home of George Semler. The eccentric fête was fine training for these children of the well-to-do, including several in black-face, who would eventually have to cope with similar social circumstances in their adult life, such as the Twelfth Night celebration at the Century Club (page 104).

Byron also photographed Semler's home and family in 1899 and 1902.

R. HOE & CO., SCHOOL FOR APPRENTICES, 1904

On June 15, 1902, this last survivor of the old apprentice system was featured in a *New York Daily Tribune* article, unearthed by Grace Mayer in her research for *Once Upon a City*. R. Hoe & Company, manufacturer of printing presses, had 300 apprentices in 1902. In order for him to become an apprentice, a boy's parents had to sign an agreement binding him to five years of work and night school. The company paid $2.50 per week for the first six months, then increased the wage annually to a maximum of $7.00 per week in the fifth year. Despite the Dickensian undertones of this forty-year-old system, the apprentices were said to gain much from their practical training and course work, which prepared them for a wide variety of career choices, including working at R. Hoe & Company for full wages, a princely $2.50 per day.

BRYANT HIGH SCHOOL — STENOGRAPHY & TYPEWRITING, 1906

The first public high school in Queens was founded in 1889 as Long Island City High School. It relocated and merged with Woodside High School in 1904, when it was renamed in honor of the renowned poet and editor William Cullen Bryant. It moved again in 1939, to 31st Avenue and 48th Street in Long Island City, where it remains today.

Patented in 1879, the stenograph was essentially a shorthand typewriter, with five keys that produced a series of dashes that represented letters of the alphabet. At the time of this photograph, training in stenography was imperative for any young woman who wanted to be employed as a secretary. Learning to read the complicated code of dashes was central to becoming an accomplished user of this odd machine.

The Sporting Life

Not all New York is sedentary, voyeuristic and pleasure-seeking.
A considerable proportion of our population expends great quantities
of energy in enthusiastic pursuit of the sporting life...

LARRY MERCHANT, 1967

THE NEW YORK SPY

The Byron Company's tenure followed on the heels of the late-nineteenth-century growth in the popularity of sports in the United States. *King's Handbook of New York* (1893), in its listings of several athletic clubs and their missions, conveys the expected physical and mental benefits of sport. For instance, the Manhattan Athletic Club was founded in 1877 "for the encouragement of athletic exercises and games, and to promote physical culture and social intercourse among its members"; the New York Athletic Club was incorporated in 1870 "for the promotion of amateur athletics, physical culture and the encouragement of all manner of sport"; and the Pastime Athletic Club was incorporated in 1891 "to encourage all out and in-door exercises, and to promote the social interests of its members." Clearly, the public perception of athletics was a positive one, and sporting events—from the 500-year-old game of curling to the recently popularized and affordable sport of cycling—were taking place all over New York City, indoors and out, in all seasons. Despite sport's broadly based popularity, most of Byron's images reflect the enjoyment of sport by the well-to-do.

In the years prior to World War I, Byron was there to document the many facets of New York's sporting life. Presumably much of this work was done on speculation, with the hope that the newspapers, in their effort to accommodate the public's thirst for the popular subject, would be willing to pay for the right image.

BASEBALL — NEW YORK'S POLO GROUNDS, 1896

THE BYRON COLLECTION, 93.1.1.14856

Known as the "Gothams" until 1885, the team that became the New York Giants played their first game on May 1, 1883, at the Polo Grounds at 110th Street between Fifth and Sixth Avenues in Manhattan. They would close out the 1880s with pennant wins in 1888 and 1889. In the early 1890s the team moved further uptown to the new Polo Grounds at 157th Street on the Harlem River, depicted here. The Polo Grounds was also home to the New York Cuban Giants, which became the first salaried professional black baseball team in 1885.

DEFENDER — COMING HOME, 1895

THE BYRON COLLECTION, 93.1.1.16528

The first ship in the world to use aluminum and manganese bronze alloys in its hull construction, *Defender* was built by the New York Yacht Club when the British *Valkyrie III* challenged the club's primacy in the Americas Cup race. *Defender* won all three races of the challenge, the final by forfeit, maintaining the New York Yacht Club's hold on the prize, a reign that would persist until its first loss in 1983 to Australia's *Australia II*.

While on board the *New York World*'s tugboat, Byron made salted-paper prints which were traced in pen and ink by an artist, who then rolled the drawings up tight and sent them via carrier pigeon to the *World*'s Park Row headquarters for timely reporting of the race.

START OF THE RACE, MANHATTAN FIELD, 1896

THE BYRON COLLECTION, 93.1.1.14979

Manhattan Field, located adjacent to the Polo Grounds at 157th Street and the Harlem River, hosted a wide variety of athletic events such as this college track meet with representation from the City College of New York, Yale, Harvard, and Princeton, among others.

HARVARD'S NEW SHELL, 1899

THE BYRON COLLECTION, 93.1.1.14900

Before increased riverside industry and the huge popularity of cycling began to chip away at the number of rowing enthusiasts in the late nineteenth century, the smooth waters of the Harlem River were often dotted with
rowers. Clubhouses of many rowing teams lined the river, including the Nassau Boat Club (depicted here) at the
foot of East 132nd Street, where it appears that Harvard's team debuted its new shell.

ROWING, HARLEM RIVER, 1895

THE BYRON COLLECTION, 93.1.1.17514

SHEEPSHEAD RACETRACK — FINISH OF RACE, c. 1894

The Coney Island Jockey Club Race Track was established in Sheepshead Bay, Brooklyn, by John Y. McKane, the man responsible for the expansion of the railroads to make the Coney Island area more accessible. In 1915 the racetrack was replaced by the Sheepshead Speedway, which in turn was demolished in 1923 when the site was divided and developed.

COLUMBIA COLLEGE GYM, 1904

THE BYRON COLLECTION, 93.1.1.3289

The popularization of calisthenics in the late nineteenth century was due in part to S. W. Mason's 1863 *Gymnastic Manual.* It associated physical vigor with the development of beauty in the human figure.

TEACHER'S COLLEGE—HANDBALL, 1904

Grace Mayer in *Once Upon a City* suggested that this commission "afforded the Byron Company one of its best compositions," an aesthetic judgment that has survived the test of time. The handball courts in this state-of-the-art physical education facility, photographed by Byron at its 1904 opening, were just one of many new amenities. In addition to the handball courts, the facility at 525 West 120th Street included a swimming pool, fencing courts, bowling alleys, a gymnasium, rowing machines, a reception room, administrative offices, and a very popular hair-drying room.

COLUMBIA — FOOTBALL, 1899–1900

THE BYRON COLLECTION, 93.1.1.15050

While the reputation of its football team may be lackluster today, Columbia University can justly claim its role as the first university to play organized football, in 1870. These confident teammates are conspicuously joined by a curious bystander.

CURLING, CENTRAL PARK, 1894

THE BYRON COLLECTION, 93.1.1.17508

When frozen over, the Central Park lake drew crowds of winter sports aficionados, including those who played the Scottish game of curling. In this contest, the 30-pound curling stones are slid along the ice toward a target, with players sweeping the ice before the moving disk to control its course. The object of the game is to come as close to the target as possible. The 500-year-old ice sport debuted as a full-medal sport at the 1998 Olympic Winter Games.

EVENING TELEGRAM CYCLE PARADE, 1896

THE BYRON COLLECTION, 93.1.1.1501

This June 6, 1896, event attracted hundreds of cycling fanatics, many in outlandish costumes, for the race up Broadway (or the Boulevard, as it was then known) from 65th Street to 108th Street, then on to Riverside Drive and around Grant's Tomb and the Claremont Inn. Here the day's winners pose for Byron's photograph at the base of the judges' stand.

A May 31, 1893, *New York Times* editorial lamented the effects of the recent popularity of cycling: "With the cheapening in the cost of bicycle riding in the public streets has come the abuse of that privilege by thousands of ignorant and loaferish individuals. Many of the bicyclists who swarm along the smooth asphalt of the Boulevard, particularly at night and on Sunday, are irresponsible and reckless young men to whom a stable keeper would not entrust a saddle horse…"

CHICAGO TO NEW YORK AUTO RACE, c. 1913

THE BYRON COLLECTION, 93.1.1.496

While information about this event is elusive, the back of the print includes some handwritten notes about the vehicle depicted. It is a 1913 Imp Cyclecar with two cylinders, 10 to 12 horsepower, and a maximum speed of 50 miles per hour. It sold new for $375. Cyclecars—simple, economical vehicles that worked on the same principles as a bicycle—were relatively new in 1913, and a New York-based cyclecar club was established in December of that year.

NEW YORK TO PARIS AUTO RACE, TIMES SQUARE, 1908

THE BYRON COLLECTION, 93.1.1.538

Cosponsored by *The New York Times* and Paris's *Le Matin*, the famed New York to Paris Automobile Race began at Times Square on February 12, 1908. According to the *Times,* more than 150,000 people packed the square to witness the departure of the six contenders for what would be "about the sternest test of the endurance of men and machines that has ever been undertaken." American, Italian, and German teams were joined by three French entries for the westward journey through Alaska, Siberia, Russia, Germany, and Belgium on their way to the Paris finish line. Piloted by Montague Roberts and George Schuster, the victorious American entry arrived in Paris with a twenty-six-day lead.

The festooned Hotel Astor — replaced by a 50-story office tower in 1969—dominates this image.

THE STAGE AND POPULAR ENTERTAINMENT

Give my regards to Broadway,
Remember me to Herald Square...

GEORGE M. COHAN, 1904

During its tenure as the foremost studio of stage photography, the Byron Company documented no fewer than 1,000 theatrical productions, leaving an unparalleled resource of vintage prints and negatives in the Museum of the City of New York's Byron Collection. Their predominance in this field gained the Byrons access to the leading men and women of the turn-of-the-century stage, whose off-stage lives were often documented by the Byron Company as well.

So prevalent was stage work in the firm's repertoire that its letterhead at the turn of the century read "The Stage is My Studio," and listed medals garnered at the Paris Exposition of 1900 for artificial lighting, artistic grouping, and stage pictures.

The Byron Company's stage work included vaudeville, burlesque, minstrelsy, and other forms of popular entertainment, with burlesque producers Weber & Fields being one of the firm's major clients. From Coney Island to Union Square, Byron captured a wide range of the city's popular entertainment venues and personalities.

**AMERICAN THEATRE,
TED MARK'S BIG SUNDAY NIGHT CONCERT, 1901–1902**

In addition to photographing hundreds of stage scenes, Byron often turned his camera 180 degrees to capture theater interiors filled to capacity. The flash of the magnesium powder surely stunned the audience, but the resulting evidence of a full house proved that a show was a hit and provided a useful promotional tool. Sunday night concerts were a popular form of entertainment, and were not subject to laws forbidding theatrical performances from taking place on the Christian Sabbath. The music presented on these occasions often had religious overtones.

THE WIZARD OF OZ, 1903

THE BYRON COLLECTION, 41.420.777

Here actor Bobby Gaylor, playing the Wizard, leads his crew of Phantom Guards in a scene from Fred R. Hamlin's musical extravaganza, *The Wizard of Oz*, based on the 1900 novel by L. Frank Baum. This original production of the American classic was the premier performance at the recently completed Majestic Theatre on January 21, 1903; it ran for 293 performances.

MAJESTIC THEATRE, 1903

One of almost ninety theater buildings documented by Byron, the Majestic's first year—1903—was a tremendous success, with such popular productions as *The Wizard of Oz* (opposite page) and *Babes in Toyland* (next page). Located at Columbus Circle, not far from the current location of Lincoln Center for the Performing Arts, it was the northernmost Broadway house at the time. Sadly, it was too far from the theater district and within five years motion pictures—not theater—were the mainstay here. Despite attempts by the Shuberts, Florenz Ziegfeld, and the Minsky family to revive the Majestic with legitimate theater, it continued to decline, and in 1954 it was demolished for wider pedestrian access to the equally unsuccessful New York Coliseum. In 1998 a plan to redevelop the site with a glass-and-steel tower was approved.

BABES IN TOYLAND, 1903

THE BYRON COLLECTION, 41.420.68

This full view of a scene on the set of the Master Toymaker's shop in the musical *Babes in Toyland* (lyrics by Glen MacDonough, music by Victor Herbert, directed by Julian Mitchell) even includes a glimpse of the orchestra. This original production of *Babes in Toyland* opened at the Majestic Theatre on October 13, 1903, and ran for 192 performances.

CASINO THEATRE, 1900

Since much of Byron's theater production work was done during dress rehearsals, and waiting for set and costume changes left idle time, he was afforded the opportunity to document the sumptuous interiors of many theaters. The Casino was erected at Broadway and West 39th Street in 1882 and stood until 1930, when it and the adjacent Knickerbocker Theatre gave way to the expanding Garment District.

BELASCO THEATRE (OLD REPUBLIC), 1902

Here Byron documented the transition of the defunct Republic Theatre into the Belasco. Built in 1900 by Oscar Hammerstein I, the Republic was taken over in 1902 by David Belasco, who remodeled it extensively and gave the theater his name. Around 1910, when Belasco moved on to other venues, the theater reverted to its original name. It continued as a legitimate house until 1932, when it became home to Billy Minsky's burlesque shows. After Mayor Fiorello LaGuardia banned burlesque in 1942, the Republic was converted into a movie theater, the Victory, and fell into decline. In 1995 the beautifully restored New Victory opened again as a legitimate theater.

ROMEO AND JULIET, 1899

THE BYRON COLLECTION, 34.271.813D

This scene is one of several captured by Byron from Charles Frohman's celebrated 1899 production of William Shakespeare's *Romeo and Juliet,* featuring turn-of-the-century belle Maude Adams as Juliet and heartthrob William Faversham as Romeo. The production opened on May 8, 1899, at Frohman's Empire Theatre at Broadway and 40th Street. The Empire was razed in 1953 to make way for an office tower.

WEBER & FIELDS: THE STICKINESS OF GELATINE, 1902

THE BYRON COLLECTION. 93.1.1.19812

The Byron Company photographed stage performances on speculation until about 1897, when burlesque producers Joseph Weber (1867–1942) and Lew Fields (1867–1941) commissioned the studio to photograph the opening
of the Imperial Music Hall at Broadway and West 29th Street. Thereafter, Byron photographed more than forty
Weber & Fields productions, and documented both of their homes as well.

Weber & Fields's burlesque often mocked contemporaneous theatrical productions.

AMERICAN ROOF GARDEN, 1898

THE BYRON COLLECTION, 93.1.1.17842

Before the advent of air conditioning, most New York theaters closed down during the summer. The first roof garden opened in 1882 atop the Casino Theater and quickly spawned a host of imitations that flourished into the 1920s when Prohibition and interior cooling systems rendered them obsolete. The American Theatre Roof Garden opened on June 19, 1893, and in 1899 the September issue of *Cosmopolitan* (which reproduced this image) estimated that the city's many roof garden theaters attracted a total of 10,000 visitors each night.

ARABIAN ACROBATS ON ROOF OF HAMMERSTEIN'S VICTORIA, 1901–1902

THE BYRON COLLECTION, 93.1.1.15700

Oscar Hammerstein built the Victoria on the site of an old stable at what is now Times Square, and soon joined the roof of his other theater — the adjacent Republic — to the Victoria, creating the Paradise Roof Garden. It began, innocently enough, with a small petting zoo (including a cow and a milkmaid), but soon Oscar's son William began hiring novelty and vaudeville acts through European agencies. After an engagement at the Paradise Roof Garden, these performers would proudly return home with the audience-drawing credit "Direct from Hammerstein's New York." The Paradise Roof Garden became increasingly sensationalistic until its 1915 demise.

A similar print in this series reads "Saad Dahdowh with Sie Nassan Ben Ali, Arabs, Pyramid Holder," suggesting that this troupe's title is literal.

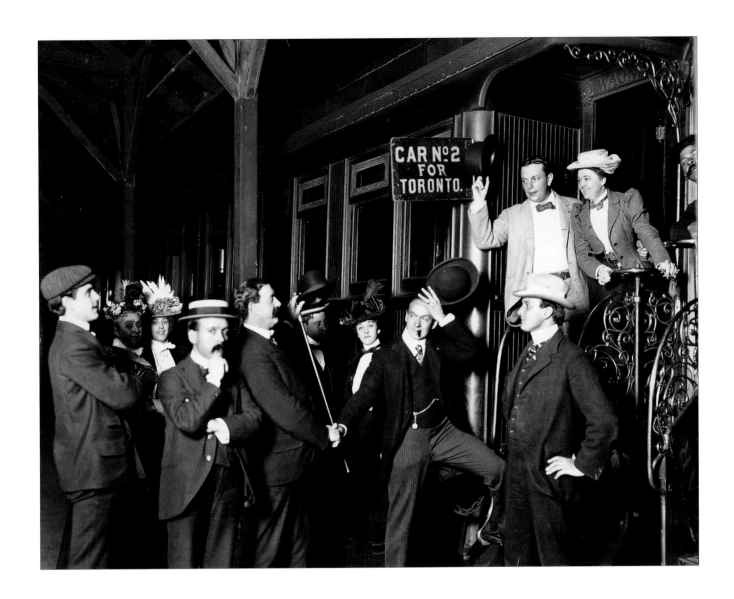

ALICE NIELSEN ON SPECIAL TRAIN TO TORONTO, 1898

THE BYRON COLLECTION, 93.1.1.9140

This publicity photograph captures operatic vocalist Alice Nielsen (1876–1943), with her manager Frank L. Perley and Eugene Cowles of her supporting cast, boarding their Toronto-bound Wagner Palace Car for the Canadian tryout of the comic opera *The Fortune Teller*. The opera met with rave reviews in Toronto and was also well received upon its New York debut a few weeks later. It had a short run in New York, but the score established Victor Herbert's reputation as a leading operetta composer.

MARIE DRESSLER'S RETURN, 1905

THE BYRON COLLECTION, 41.420.540

Seen here upon her August 5, 1905, return from a European sojourn, Marie Dressler (1869–1934) was also photographed by Byron onstage and relaxing at home. Her first New York appearance was in *The Robber of the Rhine*
(1892), and her fame in vaudeville continued for decades in England and the United States. She was known for
her hefty, shrewish appearance in comedic roles, as the title of her 1924 autobiography *The Life Story of an Ugly
Duckling* suggests.

DAVID WARFIELD, 1904–1905

THE BYRON COLLECTION. 93.1.1.9326

Born in San Francisco, David Warfield (1866–1951) found his way to New York City in the 1890s, where his career as a comedic actor—centered on caricatures of the Lower East Side Jew—flourished. His success led to many serious roles as well. Byron photographed him in several plays including *The Auctioneer* (1901), *The Return of Peter Grimm* (1911), *The Music Master* (1904), *A Grand Army Man* (1907), and at least a dozen burlesque productions by Weber & Fields.

The photographer penciled a few notes on the reverse of this print: "David Warfield's favorite corner in his drawing room. Mr. Warfield is a collector of objects of art."

ETHEL BARRYMORE, 1902–1903

THE BYRON COLLECTION, 93.1.1.8603

This casual portrait of Ethel Barrymore (1879–1959) was taken after her 1901 debut in a starring role on the New York stage as Madame Trentoni in *Captain Jinks of the Horse Marines.* Barrymore is often remembered for the line she delivered at the end of her curtain calls: "That's all there is, there isn't any more!" Byron also made portraits of her brothers John and Lionel Barrymore.

SARAH BERNHARDT, 1896

Of all the stars that Joseph Byron photographed offstage, the popular French actress Sarah Bernhardt (1844–1923) was clearly his greatest conquest. Percy Byron recalled that it took much prodding by his father to gain Ms. Bernhardt's permission to be photographed at all, but upon seeing the results of their first 15-minute shoot, she insisted that Byron photograph all of her plays—which he happily did.

This and several other portraits were taken at the fashionable Hoffman House on Broadway between 24th and 25th Streets, where Bernhardt maintained a suite of rooms. Four portraits from this session were published in the June 1896 issue of *Munsey's Magazine*.

MISS LILLIAN RUSSELL AT PROCTOR'S 23RD ST., 1905

Lillian Russell's ten-week engagement at Proctor's 23rd Street Theatre, relatively late in her career, marked her return to vaudeville after a long absence. Her $3,000-per-week stint brought much-needed income to the veteran entertainer, and her appearance was a promotional coup for Proctor's. In his review, Acton Davies of the *Sun* concluded, "Songs may come and songs may go, but age can not wither nor variety custom stale Miss Russell. She is the same old Lillian, and her voice is the same old voice."

Byron also photographed Russell (1861–1922) at home and in several other theatrical productions.

REHEARSAL — NED WAYBURN'S TOWN TOPICS, 1915

Town Topics was one of hundreds of musical reviews produced by Ned Wayburn. The director and producer began his career as an usher; he went on to sing and dance in vaudeville, originate ragtime piano with his song "Syncopated Sandy," and manage the Century Theatre.

KARSY'S GIANT MYRIPHON, 1901–1902

THE BYRON COLLECTION, 93.12.1.15812

Byron was of little help in documenting this image, penciling on the back of the print "Musical Act." The unusual contraption depicted was probably the centerpiece of a musical act at Coney Island, or at Union Square, where similar entertainment could be found.

KEITH'S BICYCLE TRACK, 1901–1902

Benjamin Franklin Keith and his partner E. F. Albee knew each other as circus men, but began a partnership in 1885 showing continuous vaudeville at the Bijou Theatre in Boston. In 1887 they opened similar theaters in Providence and Philadelphia; in 1893 they acquired the lease on New York's Union Square Theatre, probably the site of the "Bicycle Track" depicted here. Keith, as house manager, was known for his conservatism, permitting neither nudity nor innuendo in his productions, which attracted a profitable family audience. Albee handled the partnership's business affairs. Keith and Albee dominated the vaudeville circuit nationwide well into the twentieth century.

The Theatre Unique (facing page) and Automatic Vaudeville, just two blocks apart on East 14th Street, typified the popular entertainment establishments on and around Union Square at this time. From fortunetelling to burlesque peep shows, the nature of the entertainments offered can be gleaned from the titles visible in the Automatic Vaudeville photograph: *My Cosey Corner Girl; Hannah, Won't You Open that Door; An Affair of Honor;* and *South African Warriors.* The prominent "Smoking Prohibited, Offensive to the Ladies" sign establishes that these arcades catered to both men and women.

162

THEATRE UNIQUE, 1908

CONEY ISLAND—JOLLY TRIXIE AND PRINCESS WEE WEE, 1908–1909

THE BYRON COLLECTION, 93.1.1.3429

Dreamland, the site of this side show, opened at Coney Island on May 15, 1904, and immediately began to compete with its neighbors, Steeplechase Park and Luna Park, both for shows and clientele. In addition to the many amusements and side shows available at Coney Island, a variety of less wholesome delights earned the resort its nickname "Sodom by the Sea."

164

CONEY ISLAND — LEVITATION, 1908–1909

THE BYRON COLLECTION, 93.1.1.3425

LEW DOCKSTADER MINSTRELS, 1903

The *New York Times* of September 18, 1886, noted that Dockstader's Minstrel Hall had opened "amid great rejoicing" on the west side of Broadway near 29th Street. Lew Dockstader had been in the business since 1873, and his minstrel productions traveled throughout the United States.

In minstrelsy, an interlocutor would engage in banter with gaudily dressed members of the company caricaturing African Americans—usually in blackface—creating negative stereotypes that last to this day.

MUTUAL FILM CO., 1600 BROADWAY, 1918

Joseph Byron dabbled in the fledgling film industry, making a special trip to England and Paris in the late 1890s to meet various pioneers in the field, including the Lumière brothers in Paris. After purchasing equipment, and making a film of the 1897 Easter Parade on Fifth Avenue, Joseph gave up the medium as a fleeting novelty, a decision he may have regretted by the time this Byron Company photograph was taken.

Charles Chaplin was under contract with the Mutual Film Company from 1916 to 1918.

*In front of us rose the imposing sight of skyscrapers—the same skyline
we had admired so often on postcards. Many of the passengers had only
heard talk of New York and stood with their mouths open, spellbound...We
sighed as we set foot on solid ground, there, gaping before us, jaws
of the iron dragon: the immense New York metropolis.*

BERNARDO VEGA, 1914
MEMOIRS OF BERNARDO VEGA

From late-nineteenth-century steerage vessels to the luxury liners of the
1920s and 1930s, the Byron Company documented no fewer than 155
ships that passed through New York Harbor. New York's predominance as
America's gateway (74 percent of all immigrants to the United States between 1880 and
1919 went through New York City) and as a popular destination provided ample subject
matter for Byron's ship photography. The city's infrastructure played a significant role
in accommodating the great volume of vessels. From 1904 to 1909 approximately 35
miles of new wharf space were created, including 51 piers, 21 platforms, and 30 pier
extensions.

While the earlier ship commissions were presumably garnered by Joseph Byron, the mas-
sive documentation of the world's luxury liners from the late teens until the firm's 1942
closing was undertaken by Percy Byron. This specialization was so successful that the
firm's letterhead in the 1930s read "Ship Specialists" and noted that Byron held "Ten
Gold Medals and Diplomas from Principal Exhibitions of Europe and America," listing
first prize in the International Expositions of 1931 and 1932.

The Byron Collection's holdings in ship photography number some 4,000 prints and negatives, many of which have never been published. Percy Byron's mastery of composition
and technique brought this work to its highest level, and the legacy of his dedication to
this subject lives on in the Museum of the City of New York's unparalleled archive.

S.S. ETHIOPIA, 1900

The Byron Collection includes nearly one hundred prints of this transatlantic voyage of the Anchor Line's *Ethiopia*, including views with Newfoundland and Ireland in the background. These prints are 5×7 inches—a much more portable size than Byron's standard 11×14- or 8×10-inch formats. The series includes passengers in various classes of travel, and shows many parts of the ship. Several images depict the crew working in this storm. The verso of a similar print reads, "Taking in the Awning. A wet Sunday."

The *Ethiopia*, built in Scotland in 1873, undertook her maiden voyage from Glasgow to New York. She was also in New York in 1907, when she was sold for scrap.

**S.S. PATRICIA, STEERAGE NUMBERED READY TO LAND
AT ELLIS ISLAND, 1902**

Byron made 36 photographs of the S.S. *Patricia* and its passengers on their journey from Boulogne-sur-Mer, France, to New York City. Like those taken of the S.S. *Ethiopia*, these prints are 5×7 inches, reflecting the use of a relatively portable camera. Most of Byron's ship photographs were taken in or near New York Harbor, but when he did travel abroad, he seemed always to document the trip. This evocative image shows hopeful immigrants, numbered for admittance to the U.S. Immigration Station at Ellis Island, after a long transatlantic journey.

S.S. UMBRIA, c. 1897

The S.S. *Umbria* made her maiden voyage from Liverpool to New York in 1884. In 1887 she set the transatlantic speed record—six days, four hours, and forty-two minutes. She was sold for scrap in 1910.

S.S. BERGENSFJORD, NORWEGIAN AMERICA LINE, c. 1935

THE BYRON COLLECTION, 93.1.3.26

This welcoming crowd awaits the arrival of the S.S. *Bergensfjord* to its Hudson River pier. The launching and arrival of the great ocean liners along the Hudson River were festive occasions, now lost to the past.

The *Bergensfjord*, built in 1913, was a veteran of both world wars, barely escaping Norway before the German invasion of 1940, and serving out its term in Halifax, Nova Scotia. She returned to the Norwegian America Line in 1946.

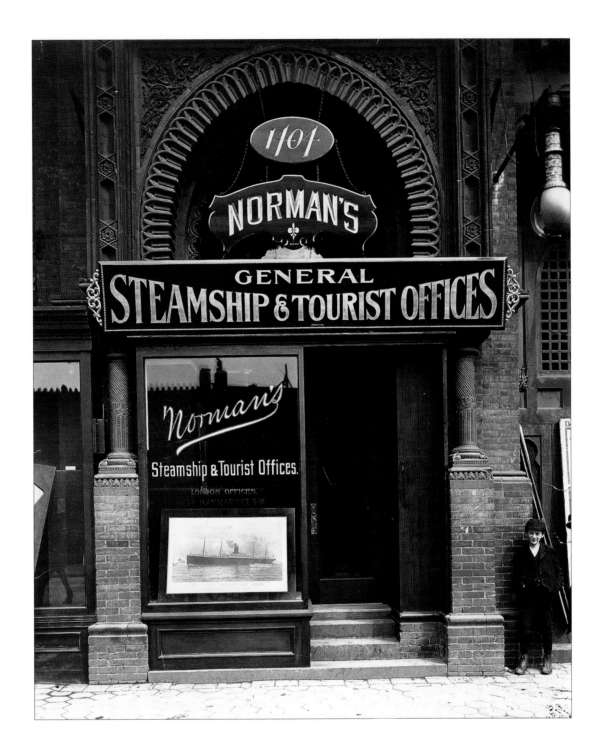

NORMAN'S STEAMSHIP AND TOURIST OFFICE, 1902

THE BYRON COLLECTION, 93.1.1.7386

Norman's Steamship and Tourist Office leased its space from the ornate Casino Theatre at Broadway and West 39th Street. The Byron Company surely came by this modest commission through its many connections in the steamship industry.

S.S. FRANCE, GRAND FOYER, 1924

THE BYRON COLLECTION, 93.1.3.11464

The sumptuous interiors of the great Atlantic liners were masterfully documented through the Byron Company's numerous steamship commissions. In this typical view, Byron captured the *France*'s rich Grand Foyer. The *France* made its maiden voyage from Le Havre to New York in 1912 and was commissioned by France in 1914 to serve as a troop and hospital ship during World War I. She returned to passenger service in 1919, was retired at Le Havre in 1932, and dismantled at Dunkirk in 1934.

S.S. NORMANDIE, 1935

More than 350 Byron images of the S.S. *Normandie* survive as a record of its maiden voyage, on which Percy Byron was the official photographer. Perhaps more than any other vessel, the $60,000,000 S.S. *Normandie* befitted the term "luxury liner." The main dining room, which boasted lalique fixtures, seated 1,000 in an area 300 feet by 43 feet by 3 stories high. The ship had a luxurious dog kennel, a theater, a chapel, a winter garden, and a 100-car garage. She was requisitioned for military use in 1941, just six years after her 1935 maiden voyage, and was gutted by fire in her New York berth in 1942. Fortunately, most of her fixtures had been removed; they continue to bring top dollar at auction.

PIER 88, CROWD ON PIER BALCONY AT SAILING OF NORMANDIE, 1936

THE BYRON COLLECTION, 93.1.3.998

S.S. NORMANDIE GYMNASIUM, CABIN CLASS, 1935

THE BYRON COLLECTION, 93.1.3.879

S.S. NORMANDIE DINING SALON LOOKING AFT, FIRST CLASS, 1935

THE BYRON COLLECTION, 93.1.1.11836

S.S. SATURNIA, POMPEIAN SWIMMING POOL, 1928

THE BYRON COLLECTION, 93.1.1.11317

The Byron Company often employed models in its commercial work, lending a touch of glamour to its promotional photographs. While the *Saturnia*'s initial route in 1927 was between Trieste and South America, service was transferred to Trieste–New York in 1928, when Byron took this and many other photographs for the Consulich Line. During World War II, the *Saturnia* was renamed the *Francis Y. Slanger* and was converted into a hospital ship by the United States. She resumed transatlantic service as the *Saturnia* in 1947.

HOISTING AEROPLANE ON S.S. PARIS, 1931

THE BYRON COLLECTION, 93.1.3.618

Launched in 1916, the *Paris*'s maiden voyage from Le Havre to New York was delayed until 1921 due to the interruption of World War I. The 764-foot-long and 85-foot-wide vessel was obviously large enough to accommodate bulky cargo—like the aircraft depicted here—in addition to its 560 first-class, 530 second-class, and 840 third-class passengers. The ship was gutted by fire and capsized at her berth in Le Havre in 1939.

EAST RIVER BRIDGE, 1898

THE BYRON COLLECTION, 93.1.1.17867

Byron appears to have perched on the bow of a ship being tugged into New York Harbor, capturing the vista of water, bridge, and skyline.

Built between 1867 and 1883, at the expense of more than twenty lives, the Brooklyn Bridge symbolizes the sheer determination of man over nature. Designed by Washington A. Roebling, the project was completed after his untimely death by his son John and his wife Emily. Its unprecedented span and graceful beauty made the bridge an instant New York City icon, a role it continues to hold to this day. The bridge made the first physical connection between the great cities of Brooklyn and New York, a connection that was politically solidified in the year of this photograph with the consolidation of the five boroughs into Greater New York.

THE PHYSICAL CITY

This is the first sensation of life in New York—you feel that the Americans have practically added a new dimension to space. They move almost as much on the perpendicular as on the horizontal plane. When they find themselves a little crowded, they simply tip a street on end and call it a skyscraper.

WILLAM ARCHER, 1900
AMERICA TODAY: OBSERVATIONS AND REFLECTIONS

Joseph Byron and his family immigrated to New York on the cusp of its transformation into one of the world's largest and most influential cities. The Byron Company witnessed and documented the vertical and horizontal growth of New York, as corporate icons rose from the soil in the form of increasingly taller skyscrapers and as the city consolidated in 1898 into a metropolis of five boroughs and nearly four million people, second in size only to London.

The Byron Company transferred its operations to New York at a propitious time, and its business prospered as a result. The city's role as the center for stage and theatrical entertainment, its consolidation of great wealth and the resulting influence in the world's markets, and its growing publishing and communications industries provided both the subject matter and the means by which the Byron Company produced its extraordinary record of New York City's built environment.

From the city's infrastructure and major public projects, to its churches, skyscrapers, and monuments, the Byron Company managed to accumulate, through a wide array of commissions and speculative work, a chronicle of New York City's physical development from the late nineteenth century through the onset of World War II.

NEW YORK YACHT CLUB, 1893

The New York Yacht Club, the oldest such organization in the country, was founded in 1844 and incorporated in 1865. In 1901 the club moved from its headquarters at 27 Madison Avenue to its current Beaux-Arts clubhouse on West 44th Street. The New York Yacht Club is most famous for its founding of the famed Americas Cup competition.

Madison Square Garden's landmark tower is visible in the near distance.

CENTRAL PARK — THE DAIRY, 1898

THE BYRON COLLECTION, 93.1.1.124268

Built in 1870, the Central Park Dairy provided fresh milk and toys to the city's children. The fairytale structure, handsomely restored in 1979, now serves as a visitor and information center.

WASHINGTON SQUARE, 1903

THE BYRON COLLECTION, 93.1.1.17995

First erected by the renowned architectural firm of McKim, Mead & White as a temporary wood-and-plaster structure for the 1889 centennial celebration of George Washington's inauguration, the Memorial Arch was so well liked that money was raised to erect this permanent version as a gateway to Washington Square. The winged figures were sculpted by Frederick MacMonnies; later sculptural additions were made by A. Stirling Calder, whose *Washington in Peace* (1918) now sits on the west pier, and by Herman A. MacNeil, whose *Washington in War* (1916) remains on the east pier. The tower visible across the square is that of the Judson Memorial Baptist Church, also designed by McKim, Mead & White (1892).

DEWEY ARCH, 1899

THE BYRON COLLECTION, 93.1.1.76872

This wood-and-plaster arch and colonnade at Madison Square was the focal point of Commodore George Dewey's triumphal procession through New York City on September 30, 1899, after defeating the Spanish forces at Manila Bay on May 1, 1898. The temporary construction, erected by the National Sculpture Society under the leadership of architect Charles R. Lamb and sculptor Frederic W. Ruckstall, was completed on September 29, just one day before the procession. The arch was intended to attract subscriptions for a permanent structure, but Dewey's popularity waned and the project was abandoned. The heavily deteriorated temporary monument was removed in late 1900.

Byron did photograph the parade itself, but also managed to capture the excitement of the event with this view of the aftermath of the parade, with hundreds of chairs strewn in the foreground.

GRACE CHURCH, 1902

An important early work of renowned Gothic Revival architect James Renwick, Jr., Grace Church (1843–1846) is one of the most significant examples of this style in America. Visible in this photograph are a portion of the church to the right, Renwick's later Grace House (1880–1881) in the center, and the rectory to the left. While Byron took full advantage of the natural late afternoon light for this composition, he added drama by inserting a more severe sky, visible overlapping the turrets, probably taken from another photograph.

ST. JOHN THE DIVINE, 1904

Heins & La Farge's design, with its Byzantine and Romanesque influences, won the architectural competition held for the Cathedral Church of St. John the Divine. Construction began in 1892, twelve years before this construction photograph. By 1911 the architects and the cathedral's original sponsor had died, leaving the partially completed structure to be redesigned in the French Gothic style so familiar to the succeeding architect, Ralph Adams Cram. Construction halted when the United States entered World War II and did not resume until 1979. Slow but steady progress continues on what will, upon completion, be the world's largest cathedral.

GRANT'S TOMB, 1903

THE BYRON COLLECTION, 93.1.1.7009

This impressive Classical Revival monument at Riverside Drive and West 122nd Street replaced a modest temporary tomb at a nearby location, a photograph of which was Percy Byron's first commercial sale, at age 15, to the *New York World*. Paid for by subscription, architect John H. Duncan's competition-winning copy of Mausoleus's Tomb at Halicarnassus in Turkey was begun six years after Grant's death in 1885. The tomb was dedicated on April 27, 1897, and in 1902 Julia Dent Grant was laid beside her husband, where they continue to rest side by side in twin black sarcophagi.

Byron left no clues about the group of men climbing the stairs. A similar composition shows the same group descending.

GRAND ARMY PLAZA, BROOKLYN, 1903

Grand Army Plaza was the heart of Brooklyn's "Gold Coast," where the homes of the well-to-do rivaled the mansions of Manhattan's Fifth Avenue. The centerpiece of the plaza is the Soldiers' and Sailors' Memorial Arch, designed by John H. Duncan. General W. T. Sherman laid the cornerstone in 1889, and the arch was completed in 1892. The 80-foot-tall structure is surmounted by a bronze quadriga by sculptor Frederick MacMonnies.

GREENWOOD CEMETERY, BROOKLYN, MAY 30, 1899 (DECORATION DAY)

Chartered in 1838, Greenwood Cemetery, with its more than twenty miles of meandering footpaths, was the place to promenade and find solitude prior to the creation of large public parks later in the century. On this auspicious 1899 Decoration Day, Byron captured the pomp and circumstance of the event, as well as the monumental grandeur of Richard Upjohn & Son's 1861 Main Entrance Gate and Gatehouse. Greenwood's over half a million permanent residents include such notable New Yorkers as William Marcy "Boss" Tweed, Samuel F.B. Morse, Henry Ward Beecher, and Lola Montez.

SPEEDWAY — BROOKLYN (OCEAN PARKWAY), 1904

THE BYRON COLLECTION, 93.1.1.18116

Brooklyn's broad Ocean Parkway was designated a Scenic Landmark in 1975 by the New York City Landmarks Preservation Commission. Designed by Frederick Law Olmstead and Calvert Vaux in the mid-1870s, it was part of an extensive system of parkways planned to connect several neighborhoods of Brooklyn with the bucolic Prospect Park.

HOTEL SHELBURNE, CONEY ISLAND, c. 1913

THE BYRON COLLECTION, 93.1.1.6690

Ocean Parkway terminated here at Seabreeze Avenue, where the Hotel Shelbourne catered to Coney Island's seasonal visitors. Built originally as the boxy Parkway Baths Hotel, allegedly in thirty days, the hotel added its many balconies and gaudy signs later, co-opting the image of the major amusement parks opening around it— Steeplechase Park (1897), Luna Park (1903), and Dreamland (1904).

STEINWAY & SONS, LONG ISLAND CITY, QUEENS, 1902

THE BYRON COLLECTION, 93.1.1.2144

German immigrant Henry Engelhard Steinway founded Steinway & Sons in a Manhattan loft on Varick Street in 1853. As it grew, the company moved to the Astoria section of Queens, where it built Steinway Village, a self-sufficient factory town with its own foundries, school, post office, parks, and employee housing. Steinway continues to manufacture pianos at this 19th Avenue and 38th Street (now Steinway Place) location, though with the addition of several buildings.

EAST 7TH STREET, 1910

This charming edifice, squeezed between its tenement neighbors, continues to grace East Seventh Street. Now occupied by St. Mary's Orthodox Church, its facade has undergone some unfortunate renovations over the years.

CITY HALL PARK LOOKING EAST TOWARD PARK ROW, c. 1899

THE BYRON COLLECTION, 93.1.1.17797

A tower of the Brooklyn Bridge peeks through an opening in the wall of buildings known as "Newspaper Row." In 1893 there were 19 daily newspapers printed in New York City, and no fewer than 15 operated, at one time or another, in this row of distinctive buildings. Several major newspaper buildings are visible; from left to right are the homes of the *World* (domed), the *Sun*, the *Tribune*, and the *Times*. By this time the *Herald*, like much of New York, had moved uptown, and the *Times* would follow in 1904. To the right of the Times Building is the Potter Building, the earliest extant edifice to use a structural steel framework. City Hall, at the lower left, seems to be undergoing one of its many cupola restorations.

TIMES BUILDING, 1904

THE BYRON COLLECTION, 93.1.1.17128

The New York Times celebrated its December 31, 1904, move into its new 25-story headquarters with a midnight fireworks display, beginning a world-famous New Year's Eve tradition. The crossroads of Broadway, Seventh Avenue, and 42nd Street, which forms the triangular plot on which the building stands, was soon dubbed Times Square, a name that has remained long after the *Times* relocated to larger quarters on West 43rd Street.

CITY HALL PARK AND BUILDINGS, c. 1917

On the eve of Lower Manhattan's pre-Depression building boom, the Singer and Woolworth towers foretold the future of this area, soon to be dotted with sky-piercing structures. Ernest Flagg's 1908 Singer Tower (facing page) was the tallest building ever demolished when it came down in 1970, and Cass Gilbert's landmark 1913 Woolworth Building remains an icon of early skyscraper design with its brilliant use of the verticality of the Gothic style. George B. Post's 1875 mansard-roofed post office (demolished 1938–1939) and City Hall stand in the shadow of the Woolworth Building.

NEW YORK SKYSCRAPERS — SINGER BUILDING, 1907

VIEW OF BROADWAY SOUTH FROM THE WOOLWORTH BUILDING, c. 1913

Byron found a new vantage point with the 1913 erection of Cass Gilbert's Gothic-inspired Woolworth Building, the tallest in the world until the Chrysler Building surpassed it in 1929. Looking south along Broadway from the intersection of Park Row, this picturesque view—taken with the "Permission of F.W. Woolworth Co."—shows St. Paul's Chapel and churchyard, the Herald Building (left foreground), and the swarming urban life that Byron so often captured at street level.

THE BRICK PRESBYTERIAN CHURCH, 1898

THE BYRON COLLECTION, 93.1.1.18012

Situated on the northwest corner of Fifth Avenue and 37th Street, this 1858 edifice supplanted its 1767 predecessor, which stood on the corner of Nassau and Beekman streets. Its interior was redecorated by John La Farge in the late nineteenth century, and the church was demolished when the congregation built a new church at Park Avenue and 91st Street in 1938.

Byron took artistic license here, adding dramatic clouds to the sky, visible overlapping the church steeple, a technique he also employed in *Grace Church* (page 187).

VIEW FROM HOTEL McALPIN, 1913

Byron pointed his camera downtown from atop the Hotel McAlpin (Broadway and 34th Street) to capture this view of the distant lower Manhattan skyline, framed by the Metropolitan Life Insurance Company tower (Napolean LeBrun & Sons, 1909) on the left, and a Wrigley's Spearmint billboard to the right.

AEOLIAN HALL, 1919

Just five years after this photograph was taken, George Gershwin debuted *Rhapsody in Blue* in Aeolian Hall with Paul Whiteman's orchestra. The concert hall occupied the main floor of the Aeolian building, but Byron chose to document the great broadcasting towers and signs atop the structure. Located at 33 West 42nd Street, the 1912 Warren & Wetmore building—redesigned in 1970 by Carl J. Petrilli & Associates—now houses the City University of New York Graduate Center.

WORLD WAR I, VICTORY CELEBRATION, 1919

Byron focused on the visceral quality of this eerie temporary monument, erected at Fifth Avenue and 59th Street for the 1919 New York City victory celebration at the close of World War I.

THE HECKSCHER BUILDING, LOOKING SOUTH
ON FIFTH AVENUE FROM 63RD STREET, 1922

THE BYRON COLLECTION, 93.1.1.14531

This 1922 glimpse down Fifth Avenue from a high floor or the roof of an apartment building at 63rd Street pre-dates both the expansive growth of midtown with such monumental structures as the Empire State Building and Rockefeller Center, and the demolition of many robber baron mansions, such as the Cornelius Vanderbilt residence (center), replaced in 1928 by the Bergdorf Goodman department store. The landmark Plaza Hotel (Henry J. Hardenbergh, 1907) at the southeast corner of Central Park frames the right edge of Byron's composition.

NIGHT SCENE, SOUTH EAST FROM 515 MADISON AVE., 1937

THE BYRON COLLECTION, 93.1.1.2054

Percy Byron made many exposures on several occasions from 515 Madison Avenue. This view incorporates, from left to right, Cross & Cross's General Electric Building (1931), Schultze & Weaver's Waldorf-Astoria Hotel (1931), William Van Allen's Chrysler Building (1930), and the New York Central Building by Warren & Wetmore (1929).

BIRD'S-EYE VIEW, BROADWAY NORTH FROM 44TH ST., 1938

THE BYRON COLLECTION, 93.1.1.5406

This view, taken from Times Square, captures New York's "Great White Way" in its pre-war heyday. The splendid Hotel Astor, demolished in 1967, occupies the foreground. The marquee of Loew's State Theater lists Claudette Colbert and Gary Cooper in *Bluebeard's 8th Wife*, and Seventh Avenue takes the eye to its termination at Central Park South, lined with towering hotels.

R.C.A. BUILDING FROM 444 MADISON, 1938

THE BYRON COLLECTION. 93.1.3.1195

Often emulated, but never equaled, Rockefeller Center is world-renowned for both its intrinsic and urban architectural design. In the design by the Associated Architects (Reinhard & Hofmeister; Corbett, Harrison & MacMurray; Raymond Hood, Godley & Fouilhoux), office buildings, theaters, stores, and the famous ice-skating rink and promenade combine to create a financial and social success, but the center's understated design is the aesthetic brilliance that underlies the complex. The centerpiece, the 70-story RCA Building (now General Electric), completed in 1933, is surrounded by several smaller office towers, with open spaces and works of art — including Paul Manship's *Prometheus* — strategically placed throughout.

CANADA DRY BUILDING, 1940

THE BYRON COLLECTION. 93.1.1.16763

The charming Joe-Harry Diner is dwarfed by Canada Dry's plant in this image of pre-war industrial Manhattan. The Canada Dry Company began in Toronto, Ontario, in 1890. Its product—Pale Dry Ginger Ale—was first shipped to New York in 1919, and two years later, the first Canada Dry plant in the United States opened on West 38th Street. In 1930, ten years prior to Byron's photograph of its 12th Avenue and West 55th Street facility, Canada Dry introduced tonic water, club soda, and collins mix.

REFERENCES

Numerous references facilitated the caption research for *Gotham Comes of Age,* including the Museum of the City of New York's archives, clipping files, and New York City land maps. The following list includes additional resources that were particularly helpful.

Armbruster, Eugene L. *Coney Island.* New York: Armbruster, limited edition, 1924.

Baragwanath, Albert K. *New York Life at the Turn of the Century in Photographs by Joseph Byron.* Museum of the City of New York and Dover Publications, Inc., 1985.

Barrett, R. *The Changing Years as Seen from the Switchboard,* 1936.

Bordman, Gerald. *American Musical Theatre, A Chronicle.* New York: Oxford University Press, 1978.

Bordman, Gerald. *The Oxford Companion to the American Theatre.* New York: Oxford University Press, 1984.

Brandinger, Edith. Research file on oyster boats prepared for Berenice Abbott's *Changing New York* photographic project, 1937, Museum of the City of New York.

Bullock, Edna Dean. From the *Debaters Handbook Series, The Employment of Women: Selected Articles.* Minneapolis, Minnesota: Wilson, 1911.

Cudahy, Brian J. *Back and Over: The History of Ferry Boats in New York Harbor.* New York: Fordham University Press, 1990.

Dommett, William Erskin. *Aeroplanes and Airships.* London: Wittaker, 1915.

Durkee Family Newsletter, Summer 1983, Vol. II, No. 2. Society of Genealogy of Durkee, 1982.

Gardner, Edward. *Erie Railroad, A Pictorial Review* Vol. 1. Philadelphia, Pennsylvania: F. Wilkes-Barre, 1975.

Goldstone, Harman H. and Martha Dalrymple. *History Preserved: A Guide to New York City Landmarks and Historic Districts.* New York: Simon & Schuster, 1974.

Gordon, John Steel. *The Scarlet Woman of Wall Street: Jay Gould, Jim Fisk, Cornelius Vanderbilt, The Erie Railroad Wars and the Birth of Wall Street.* New York: Weidenfeld and Nicholson, first edition, 1988.

Green, Harvey. *Fit for America: Health, Fitness, Sport and American Society.* New York: Pantheon Books, 1986.

Green, Stanley. *Encyclopedia of the Musical. Guide to over 2000 performers, composers, directors, productions and songs of the musical stage in London and New York.* London: Macmillan, 1976.

Hart, F. *The Story of Manhattan Beach.* New York, 1879.

Henderson, Mary. *The City and the Theatre; The History of New York Playhouses, a 235-year Journey from Bowling Green to Times Square.* Clifton, New Jersey: James T. White and Co., 1973.

Hughes, Glenn. *A History of the American Theatre 1700–1950.* Binghamton, New York: Vail-Ballou Press Inc., 1951.

Hughes, John Scott. *Famous Yachts.* London: Methuen and Co. Ltd., 1928.

Jackson, Kenneth T., ed. *The Encyclopedia of New York City.* New Haven, Connecticut: Yale University Press, 1995.

King, Moses. *King's Handbook of 1893.* New York: Benjamin Bloom International Publications, second edition, 1972.

Lancaster, Clay. *New York Interiors at the Turn of the Century, 131 Photographs by Joseph Byron.* New York: Museum of the City of New York and Dover Publications, Inc., 1976.

Mantle, Burns and Garrison P. Sherwood, eds. *The Best Plays of 1899–1909.* New York: Dodd, Mead and Company, 1933.

Mayer, Grace M. *Once Upon a City: New York from 1890 to 1910 as Photographed by Byron.* New York: Macmillan, 1958.

Miller, William H (Jr.). *The Great Luxury Liners 1927–1954; A Photographic Record.* New York: Dover Publications, Inc., 1981.

Morrow, Willie L. *400 Years Without a Comb.* California: Black Publishers of San Diego, 1973.

Myron, Matlaw, ed. *American Popular Entertainment: Papers and proceedings of the conference on the history of American Popular Entertainment.* Connecticut: Greenwood Press, 1977.

New York Telephone Company. *An Ideal Occupation for Young Women* (pamphlet), c. 1915.

Patterson, Jerry E. *Fifth Avenue: The Best Address.* New York: Rizzoli, 1998.

Simon, George T. *The Big Bands.* New York: Collier-Macmillan London, 1967.

Smith, E. W. George. *Passenger Ships of the World.* Boston: H. Dean Company, 1963.

Stern, Robert A., Gregory Gilmartin, and John Massengale. *New York 1900.* New York: Rizzoli, 1983.

Stokes, I. N. Phelps. *The Iconography of Manhattan Island,* Vol. V, 1498–1909. New York: Robert H. Dodd, 1926.

United States Food Administration. *10 Lessons in Food Conservation* (pamphlet), 1918.

Weeks, Lyman Horice, ed. *Prominent Families in New York.* New York: The Historical Company, 1897.

Whorton, James. *Crusaders for Fitness: The History of American Health Reformers.* Princeton, New Jersey: Princeton University Press, 1982.

Willensky, Elliot and Norval White. *AIA Guide to New York City.* New York: Harcourt Brace Jovanovich, 1988.

WPA Guide to New York City. New York: The New Press, 1992. First published in 1939 by the Guilds Committee for Federal Writers' Publications, Inc.

Zander, Jonas Gustaf Wilhelm. *Mechanical Exercise: A Means of Cure.* London: Churchill, 1883.

Zeisloft, Idell. *The New Metropolis.* New York: Appleton & Co., 1899.

INDEX